The I: Cornerstones of Magickal Practice

Volume Two

Poetry of the Spheres

Qabalah

Robin Fennelly

The Inner Chamber

Volume Two

Poetry of the Spheres

Poetry of the Spheres is the second book in The Inner Chamber Series

All rights reserved. No part of this book may be reproduced or transmitted in any form or by any means, electronic or mechanical, including photocopying, recording or by any informational retrieval system without permission in writing from the author except for brief quotes used in reviews or scholarly work.

Copyright © 2012 by Robin Fennelly

ISBN 978-1-257-86963-3

Cover Art: Caitlin Fennelly, M.F.A.
Illustrations and Graphics: Robin Fennelly

Bound and Printed in the United States

Dedication

In dedication to my Mother, Jeanne who provided a loving home and open environment to explore the varied spiritual paths.

In dedication to my Husband, Ned who has supported my dreams and encouraged me to pursue my chosen path.

In dedication to my five wonderful Children, Kyle, Jenny, Eryn, Caitlin and Jessica who taught me patience and nurturing and allowed me the privilege of helping them find their own destinies.

In dedication to the Elders and community of like minded Spirits that is The Assembly of the Sacred Wheel where I have learned, taught and grown.

In dedication to the Adepts and many fine Teachers of the diverse Spiritual Paths, who are I am honored to call Friend and who live the Truth that all Paths lead to the One.

Table of Contents

Introduction	9
Part Two: An Introduction to the Tree of Life	**13**
Introduction to the Tree of Life	15
Part Two: The Spheres of the Tree of Life	**31**
Chapter One: Malkuth	35
Chapter Two: Yesod	46
Chapter Three: Hod	60
Chapter Four: Netzach	74
Chapter Five: Tiphareth	88
Chapter Six: Geburah	105
Chapter Seven: Chesed	119
Chapter Eight: Binah	137
Chapter Nine: Chokmah	152
Chapter Ten: Kether	170
Chapter Eleven: Da'at, The Hidden Path	185
Part Three: Pathworkings Within the Tree	**197**
How to use the Pathworkings	199
The Sphere of Malkuth	201
The Sphere of Yesod	204

The Sphere of Hod	208
The Sphere of Netzach	213
The Sphere of Tiphareth	220
The Sphere of Geburah	224
The Sphere of Chesed	227
The Sphere of Binah	232
The Sphere of Chokmah	235
The Sphere of Kether	244
The Hidden Path of Da'at	251

Appendices	**255**
Appendix One: A Quick Study of Numbers	257
Appendix Two: The 32 Keys of Wisdom	259

Bibliography	**261**

Illustrations

Figure 1: The Spheres of the Tree — *16, 33*

Figure 2: The Three Veils — *17*

Figure 3: The Four Worlds of Expression — *19*

Figure 4: The Tetragrammaton — *21*

Figure 5: The Three Pillars of Expression — *22*

Figure 6: Three Triangles of Interaction — *23*

Figure 7: The Way of Evolution — *24*

Figure 8: The Way of Involution — *25*

Figure 9: Blank Tree — *28*

Figure 10: Location on the Tree: Yesod — *52*

Figure 11: Apex of Point: Yesod — *53*

Figure 12: Location on the Tree: Hod — *65*

Figure 13: Paths of Emanation: Hod — *66*

Figure 14: The Polarized Field: Netzach — *79*

Figure 15: Wisdom-Universal Law — *80*

Figure 16: Rays of Expression: Netzach — *81*

Figure 17: Synthesis of Energy: Tiphareth — *91*

Figure 18: Kundalini and Tiphareth — *93*

Figure 19: Location on the Tree: Tiphareth — *95*

Figure 20: The Eight Paths: Tiphareth — *96*

Figure 21: Location on the Tree: Geburah — *110*

Figure 22: Choice and Free Will: Geburah — *111*

Figure 23: The Energetic Triad: Geburah — *112*

Figure 24: Location on the Tree: Chesed   *125*

Figure 25: Gateway to the Supernals: Chesed   *126*

Figure 26: Womb of Manifestation: Chesed   *127*

Figure 27: Square of Foundation: Chesed   *128*

Figure 28: Movement From Hod: Chesed   *130*

Figure 29: Pinnacle of the Sphere: Binah   *143*

Figure 30: Fire of the Supernals: Binah   *144*

Figure 31: Force and Form: Binah   *144*

Figure 32: Womb of Manifestation: Binah   *145*

Figure 33: Location on the Tree: Chokmah   *158*

Figure 34: Point of Destiny: Chokmah   *159*

Figure 35: Womb of Manifestation: Chokmah   *160*

Figure 36: The Manifest Flow: Chokmah   *161*

Figure 37: The Tetragrammaton: Chokmah   *162*

Figure 38: The Three Veils of Negative Existence: Kether   *174*

Figure 39: The Pillar of Equilibrium: Kether   *179*

Figure 40: Point of Union: Da'at   *188*

Figure 41: The Energetic Component   *189*

Figure 42: The Gateway of Da'at   *190*

INTRODUCTION

About The Series

Poetry of the Spheres is the second volume in the series **The Inner Chamber**. These books are meant to serve as glimpses into the cornerstones of a well-structured magickal practice. The topics that will be covered in each volume comprise the basic information that should be incorporated into a diverse and well-rounded study of magick and the related arts.

Each subject will be referenced through poetry, prose and pathworkings or suggested exercises in accord with the specific material. These books are not meant to serve as an in depth study, but rather to whet the appetite for more thorough exploration as you are called and feel resonance to.

About Volume Two

Poetry of the Spheres gives the reader an overview of the Qabalistic Tree of Life through the lens of the Western Mystery Tradition. The viability of overlay of this system of information is proven in its effects and insights gained when applied to a sound magickal practice. Working with the specific energies of the individual and collective Sephirotic (of the Spheres) Paths and their Connecting Paths of Synthesis provides a greater depth of knowledge and opening to true wisdom.

This book is separated into Three Parts. **Part One** provides an introduction to the core concepts and structure of the Qabalistic Tree. This section can be referenced as you move through each of the Sephirotic spheres.

Part Two gives insight into the energies of each of the specific Sephirah. Each chapter is dedicated to a single sphere and is formatted to include:
- The Lesson of the Sphere, containing keywords and information about the core energy of that particular sphere.
- The Element of the Sphere and Numerical Value (not to be confused with Gematria) is a look at the sphere's energy relating to the attributes of numerology.
- The Location on the Tree.
- The Spiritual Experience and the Illusion of the Sphere.
- The Briatic Color, Element of the Sphere and the Magickal Image associated with each.
- The Expression of the sphere's energy within each of the Four Worlds of the Tree.

Each chapter concludes with The Living Tree; suggested activities to be used for personal study of the specific spheres. Activities may include:
- Journaling
- Meditative Focus
- Active Engagement

Part Three contains Eleven Pathworkings, each relating to a specific sphere. These can be used in future studies or stand alone as a meditative tool to open yourself to the singular energies of each sphere.

And, finally the **Appendices** at the back of the book provides a snapshot of the keywords associated with the study of numbers and a table giving information about the 32 Paths of the Tree of Wisdom. Please take a look at the **Bibliography** for some excellent resources to deepen your study.

You will find that the teachings of the Qabalah become an examination of your world and all the components and nuances that comprise your place within it. Internalizing the Paths of the Tree and then making use of their energies to guide, inform and transform your inner and outer workings is the work of a lifetime(s). And, if you commit to this work, you will be amazed at the treasures you unearth in your SELF…… RCF

Part One

An

Introduction to the Tree of Life

An Introduction to The Tree of Life
The Mystery of Qabala(h)

The Deeper meaning of the Qabalistic **Tree of Life** is a study that becomes a journey into the spiritual and mystical nature of ourselves, our world and all that is of this Cosmos. There are two basic distinctions between the Jewish Mystical Kabbalah and the Western Mystery system of the Qabalah. The difference in spelling is generally the first clue as to which system is being used. The Tree of Life, itself, remains the same within each; but, the approach and the energies, correspondences and analogies made are what become a purely Jewish Mystical perspective or one with occult roots.

Within the Jewish Kabbalah, the Ten (10) Sephiroth are ten essences referring to the 10 aspects of the Divine God. The importance of the naming of that God and the vibration of tone and sound related to that "naming" are of most importance to this system.

Within the Western Mystery Qabalah, the Ten (10) Sephiroth relate to aspects of consciousness, the macrocosm, the microcosm, the greater Universe or the totality of creation in correspondence with the Human Being.

The **Tree of Life** describes the descent of the Divine into the manifest world, and methods by which divine union may be attained in this life. It can be viewed as a map of the human psyche and of the workings of creation, both manifest and un-manifest. The story of the creative action of manifestation could be described in this way:

In the beginning there was nothing (Ayin); and as the nothing became aware of itself it also realized the limitlessness (Ayin Soph) of its being. This realization expanded and with more awareness came the birthing of limitless light (Ayin Soph Aur). This limitless light felt the urge to create and from it emanated

Divine Intelligence – Kether. All things needing balance and in its wisdom Kether divided itself and from this source of being the remaining nine spheres became emanations of wisdom, understanding, mercy, might, beauty, victory, glory, foundation and finally came to rest in the Kingdom of Earth- Malkuth.

These emanations are assigned specific attributes, each expressed both singularly and simultaneously within each of the remaining spheres.

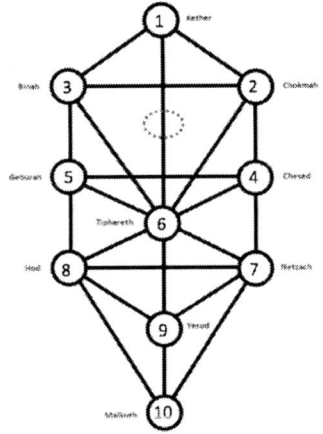

Fig. 1

The Spheres of the Tree of Life

1- Kether	The Crown	Union with God
2- Chokmah	Wisdom	Vision of God
3- Binah	Understanding	Vision of Sorrow
4- Chesed	Mercy	Vision of Love
5- Geburah	Might	Vision of Power
6- Tifareth	Beauty	Vision of Harmony
7- Netzach	Victory	Vision of Beauty
8- Hod	Glory	Vision of Splendor
9- Yesod	Foundation	Vision of the Workings of the Universe
10- Malkuth	Kingdom	Vision of the Holy Guardian Angel

The Three Veils

The three veils reside above the tree and represent the levels of non-existence just prior to creative force.

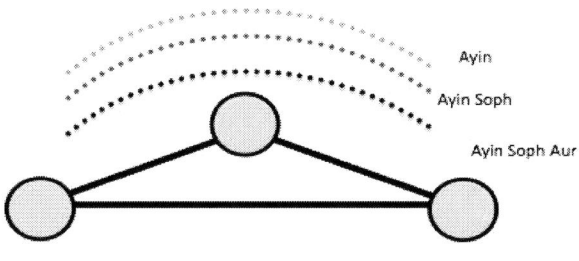

Fig. 2

Ayin is literally translated as "nothing" and is the highest and furthest away from Kether. It is the complete absence of existence.

Ayin Soph, the middle veil emanates from Ayin and translates as "no limit". It is force that is formless and without container or vessel.

Ayin Soph Aur is the closest veil to the Tree itself and emanates from the limitless nature of Ayin Soph. It means "limitless or eternal light". Within this veil there is light to serve as catalyst for recognition of the "nothing". Within this veil there is the spark needed to fuel the creative urge to create and make manifest. Now, there is also the beginnings of what will spill forth into Kether and move through the further emanations towards Malkuth.

10 Sephiroth (Spheres) of Emanation

The Sephiroth are Pure States of Being and act as vessels to contain the Divine energy that spills forth from the God-Head of Kether (being the highest expression of the Divine) down into Malkuth, the densest and manifest physical world of the Divine. The spheres at the top of the tree are lighter and more refined in their energy; more transparent and expressive of pure Light. As the energy emanates down the tree each sphere gains more density and less clarity of brilliance of light until we come to rest in the earth plane of Malkuth. Each sphere has both an English and Hebrew name and countless correspondences attributed to each.

Keywords of the Spheres

1-Kether	The Crown- The Crown Of Attainment- The 'Cause Of Causes"- The Unknowable- The Mystical Consciousness
2-Chokmah	Wisdom- The Word Of God- True Will Untainted By The Material Nature- The Radiant Consciousness
3-Binah	Understanding- The Great Sea- Absolute Belief- The Sanctified Consciousness
Da'at	*The Abyss That Holds The Key To Transformation Through The Dark Night Of The Soul This Sphere Does Not Have A Number On The Tree And Is Often Called The "Hidden Or Occult" Path*
4-Chesed	Mercy- Majesty- The Place Of Greater Awareness And Pure Compassion-The Settled Consciousness
5-Geburah	Might- Severity- Strength And Justice- Excision- Necessary Cutting Away- The Rooted Consciousness
6-Tiphareth	Beauty- Sacrifice- The Receptive Place Of The Emanations From Kether- The Transcendental Influx Consciousness
7-Netzach	Victory- The Beauty Of Nature- The Hidden Consciousness
8-Hod	Glory- Splendor- The Sphere Of Science And Craft- The Analytical Nature And Communicative Learning- The Perfect Consciousness
9-Yesod	The Foundation- Sphere Of The Subconscious- The Lunar Gates- Dreams And Illusion - The Astral - The Pure Consciousness
10-Malkuth	The Kingdom- The Plane Of Physical Existence- Manifest Reality- The Elements And All Of Manifest Life- The Scintillating Consciousness

22 Additional Paths (32-inclusive of the Spheres)

The Paths connect the Sephiroth and act as conduits, filters and refiners of the energies of the connecting spheres. Just as the Spheres are States of Being, these are the Paths of "becoming" those pure states of being. The 22 Paths with the 10 Spheres (often referred to as Paths as well) are considered the *32* Keys of Wisdom.

Numerology note: 3+2=5 the master number of the Hierophant Tarot card- the energy of the Pentagram and the ultimate state of disruptive force that is both transformative and transmutive.

Please see Appendix Two for a table of the 32 Paths.

The Four Worlds of Expression

There are four realms (worlds) of existence within which the Tree of Life is contained. Each world emanates one to the other; from the highest and most refined energy at the place of Atziluth to the densest realm in Assiah. The Four Worlds describe the creative process and each has a section of the Tree contained within its individual realms. Concurrently, as in all viable esoteric systems, the entirety of the Tree itself is also contained simultaneously within each of the worlds. Thus, each sphere exists in All Four Worlds.

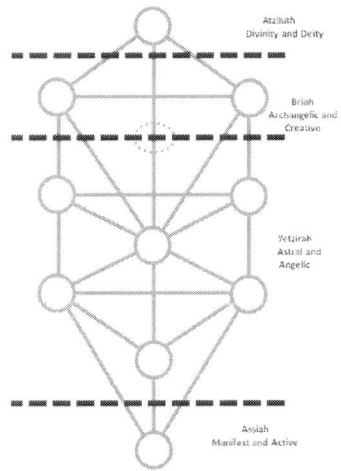

Fig. 3

Atziluth　　*World of Origin (FIRE)*

World of Archetypes　　The Spiritual World. Home to the energies of the Gods/Goddesses. This is the place of the creative urge of Deity to move beyond itself and make manifest something more. This is the place of the un-knowable and un-nameable Source of All. The realm of causes and the home of the Divine names reside here.

Briah　　*The World of Creation (WATER)*

Creative/ Archangelic World　　The Soul/or Higher SELF is expressed here. The Archangels reside in this world. This is the realm of Ideas of the highest order. This is the Idea of the manifest world before it is actually brought into being. This is also the world through which the initial study of Qabalah is often begun. Briatic colors are the standard designation for the spheres and it is through this world that clarity and greater communication between man and the Higher Self are realized and acted upon.

Yetzirah　　*The World of Formation (AIR)*

Astral/Angelic World　　The Mental Plane. This is the stuff of the Astral and as such is the world of formation. The place of the collective unconscious and Anima Mundi (world soul). This is the realm where specific forms are created. The Angels of the Qabalah reside here.

Assiah　　*World of Manifestation (EARTH)*

Active/Material World　　The Physical World. Planetary and Elemental energies are assigned at this level. This is the world in which we feel most comfortable and can identify with the energies most clearly, although we probably know the least about the hidden nature of this world in terms of actual working knowledge. This is the place of knowing "oneself".

The Hebrew Letters and The Aleph-Beth

The Hebrew alphabet is called the Aleph-Beth. The letters are read right to left when combined as words. Each of the 22 Hebrew Letters is assigned to a specific Path and has multiple meanings associated with it. Each also carries the energy of a specific word associated with it. When used in conjunction with the attribute of the Path on which it is placed, there is a greater depth of esoteric knowledge to be gained.

The individual spheres are assigned a combination of these letters to form a specific name for that sphere. The paths connecting Tiphareth, Chesed and Chokmah form The **Tetragrammaton, the Sacred Name of God.** The collective energy of the three individual letters placed in conjunction with the others interact in a way that issues forth the power of the spoken word of creation.

Yod-Heh-Vau-Heh

Fig. 4

Additionally, each of the letters has a numeric value which gives greater meaning to the combining of letters to create words. This is the practice of ***Gematria***; the numeric values of the letters of a word are added together and believed to bear relation to other words that have the same numeric value. This method is used as a method of blessing someone either by the numeric value of a name, date or birthday with a number that relates to a positive quality such as *light, life* or other.

For the purposes of this book, I will be using the tool of Numerology for comment on the Path number of each of the spheres. In each chapter, this will be designated as the **Numerical Value.**

Three Pillars of Expression

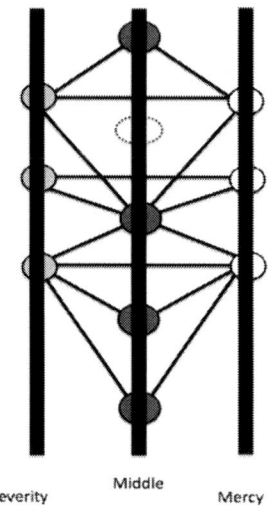

Fig. 5

The Pillar of Severity: Feminine- Providing the necessary Form and Restriction (contractions prior to Birth). The spheres of this pillar are: **Binah- Geburah and Hod.**

The **Middle** (equalizer) **Pillar:** The place of balance where the Greater Work is synthesized. This is the place of the rising Kundalini, the lunar and the solar pathways combined and the greater knowledge of Life, Death and Rebirth. This is the catalyst (The Serpent of Wisdom) for evolution of the Soul and the **Pillar of Consciousness** in its ascent. In its descent from Kether to Malkuth, the Path of Involution, it becomes the **Pillar of Grace**. The Spheres of this pillar are: **Kether-Tiphareth-Yesod and Malkuth.**

The Pillar of Mercy: Masculine- Providing the necessary Force and Expansion (the seed planted). The spheres of this pillar are: **Chokmah- Chesed and Netzach.**

Three Triangles of Interaction

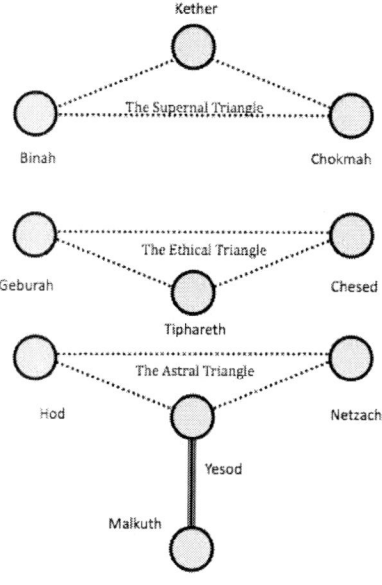

Fig. 6

The Three Triangles express the dynamics and interaction of a triune of specific spheres and the three states of impulse, active momentum and the synthesized will of creative expression.

The Supernal Triangle represents the Primal State of Being. This is the Triad of Creation:

Kether	The Urge
Chokmah	The Male Flow of Seed
Binah	The Female Womb of Form

The Ethical Triangle represents the Actions towards viability:

Chesed	The Sum Total of Its Parts
Geburah	The Necessary Culling and Filtering
Tiphareth	The Catalytic Fire or Generator

The Astral Triangle represents Mind/Heart connected by Will:

    Hod   Pure Inventive Mind
    Netzach   Pure Creative Fire
    Yesod   Determiner of Manifestation or Dream State

The Lightning Flash

The Lightning Flash is the sequence in which the energies of the Sephiroth emanate from one to the other. The path moves in action of ascent and descent through the Tree, enlivening each of the spheres and connecting paths in turn with synthesized and focalized energy.

The Way of Evolution follows the ascent from Malkuth to Kether, moving from the physical plane towards that of the Limitless **All**.

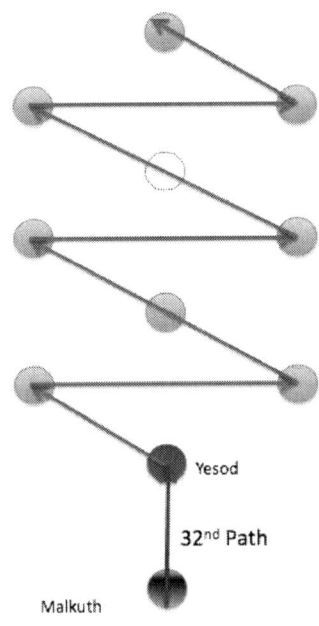

Fig. 7

The Way of Involution is the descent from Kether to Malkuth. This is the pattern of manifestation, moving from a place of formlessness towards the densest and most manifest place of existence.

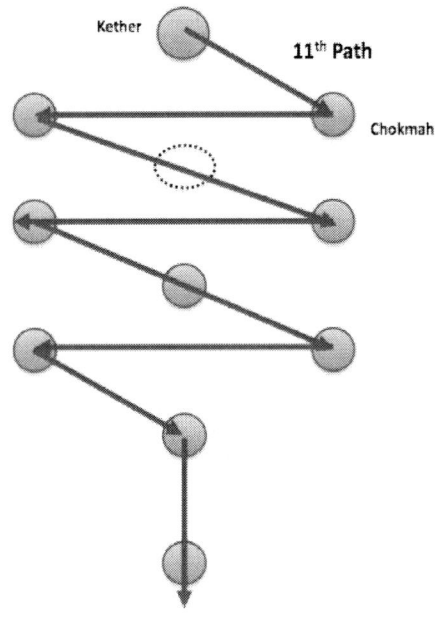

Fig. 8

The Colors of the Spheres

Each of the spheres is assigned four colors in accord with which of the Four Worlds that sphere's energy is correlating to. In some readings you will find them identified by the nomenclature of a Royal Scale.

The King Scale, which correlates to the Divine World of Atziluth.

The Queen Scale, which correlates to the Archangelic World of Briah.

The Prince Scale, which correlates to the Angelic World of Yetzirah. This color is a combination of the King and Queen Scale colors of the sphere. In this way, you could think of Divinity (Atziluth) sending forth its Divine Messenger (Archangel of Briah) to command and guide the work to be done by the Angels (Yetzirah) that will extend into manifest creation (Assiah).

The Princess Scale, which correlates to the Manifest World of Assiah. This color is the deepest hues and tones of the combination of the colors preceding it. This is also the densest form of those combined colors and they are often flecked with the specific hue of light corresponding to the King or Queen scale of colors.

Table of the Sephirotic Colors

Sphere	Atziluth King	Briah Queen	Yetzirah Prince	Assiah Princess
Kether	Brilliance	White Brilliance	White Brilliance	White flecked with Gold
Chokmah	Soft Powder Blue	Gray	Blue Pearl Grey	White flecked with Red, Blue and Yellow
Binah	Crimson	Black	Dark Brown	Grey flecked with Pink
Da'At *The Hidden Sphere*	Lavender	Silvery Grey	Pure Violet	Grey flecked with Gold
Chesed	Deep Violet	Blue	Deep Purple	Deep Azure flecked with Yellow

Sphere	Atziluth King	Briah Queen	Yetzirah Prince	Assiah Princess
Geburah	Orange	Scarlet	Bright Scarlet	Red flecked with Black
Tiphareth	Clear Pink Rose	Golden Yellow	Salmon	Golden Amber
Netzach	Amber	Emerald Green	Bright Yellowish Green	Olive flecked with Gold
Hod	Violet Purple	Orange	Russet Red	Yellowish Brown flecked with Gold
Yesod	Indigo	Violet	Very Dark Purple	Citrine flecked with Azure
Malkuth	Yellow	Russet Citrine Olive Black	Black Russet Citrine Olive flecked Gold	Black with rays of Olive and Yellow

Blank Tree to Color

One of the best ways to assist with a deeper understanding of the Tree is to use a blank tree and label and color each of the spheres in accord with their scale. Make four copies of the Tree on the next page and then color each of the spheres to correspond with each of the Four Worlds of Atziluth, Briah, Yetzirah and Assiah. Color one sphere at a time as you move through this book.

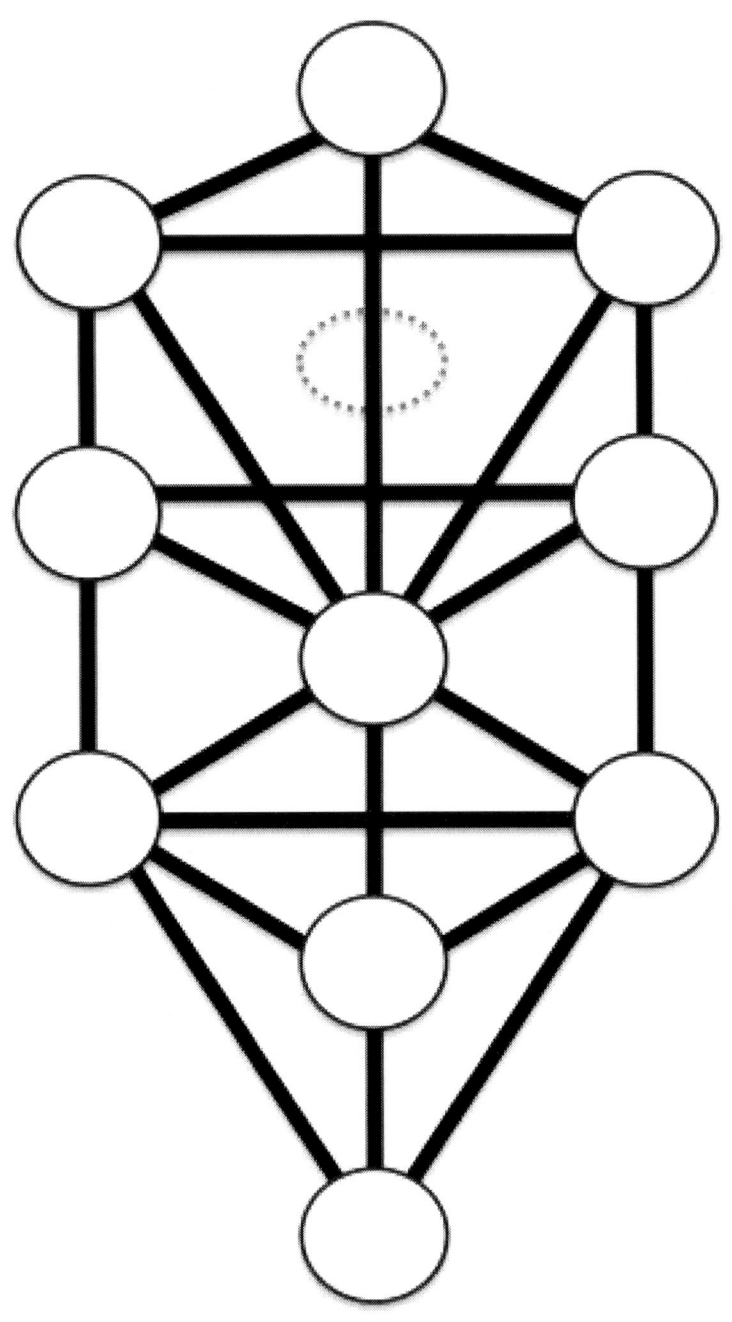

Fig. 9

28

Living the Tree

The first consideration for effectively incorporating the Tree into daily practice and mundane life is that of visualizing the Tree as multi-dimensional. It is a living construct that resides in all time and space, simultaneously, and is not a flat landscape. Additionally, there is held within each of the individual Sephirah a complete Tree, inclusive of all of the Sephiroth. Again, this construct is multi-dimensional in nature. And, continuing with this thought, another complete Tree resides within each of the subsets of a sphere; thus, replicating ad infinitum.

The focus of most ritual work is upon the intent of lifting the participants into the lower realms of Yesod; that being the interface that can be used most effectively. For truly, anything above this plane moves us further and further away from our ability of literal comprehension. The semantics of description of these realms put forth are simply that, and are the attempt at trying to take something that is essentially incomprehensible more easy to wrap our minds around. The way of human nature is to aspire towards that which is unknown and greater than ourselves. So, it is with this thought in mind that we pursue the study of the higher spheres and make ready the way for our deeper understanding in accord with our spiritual growth and evolution. Entering into Qabalistic study with this information, will provide a deeper perspective and different approach that can then be applied in a practical way.

So, how would one apply this vast body of knowledge to a spiritual or mundane practice? Although undertaking a study of the Qabala can seem daunting just in the sheer amount of information associated with each of the spheres and paths it is a system that can be overlaid on any viable esoteric or mundane pursuit.

For example, each night as we retire for a good night's sleep and enter the world of dreams, we are in effect traveling from Malkuth (the physical manifest world) into Yesod (the world of dreams, the astral, memories and the subconscious). When we have that flash of inspiration we have moved into the realm of Hod (mind, intellect and first beginnings of invention). And, when we are moved to a place of love and beauty, we have touched upon the essence of Netzach (the sphere of Venus and emotional outpour). In our moments of feeling the most courageous and enlivened we are drawing on the energy of Tiphareth (sphere of the Sun and sacrifice). When anger moves us towards release of what no longer serves, we have touched upon Geburah (transformation through release). And, when we forgive those who have wronged us because we can see from a clearer perspective we are employing the energies of Chesed (the sphere of mercy founded on unconditional love). If we take a leap of faith and allow our hidden selves to see the light held within each, we have crossed the abyss of Da'at. In our most nurturing creative moments bourne on wings of deep insight we have connected with Binah (the Great Mother and primal womb) and when we put aside our own desires, ego and needs and we are able to see from a greater vantage point the needs of others we have embraced Chokmah (the sphere of wisdom of the Cosmos). And, in those private and personal moments when we feel we have reached into the very depths of our Higher nature and see the brilliance of our own Divinity reflected back in the radiant being of another, we have opened to the downpour of Kether (the Godhead, Crown of Source and All Knowing).

Part Two

The Spheres of the Tree

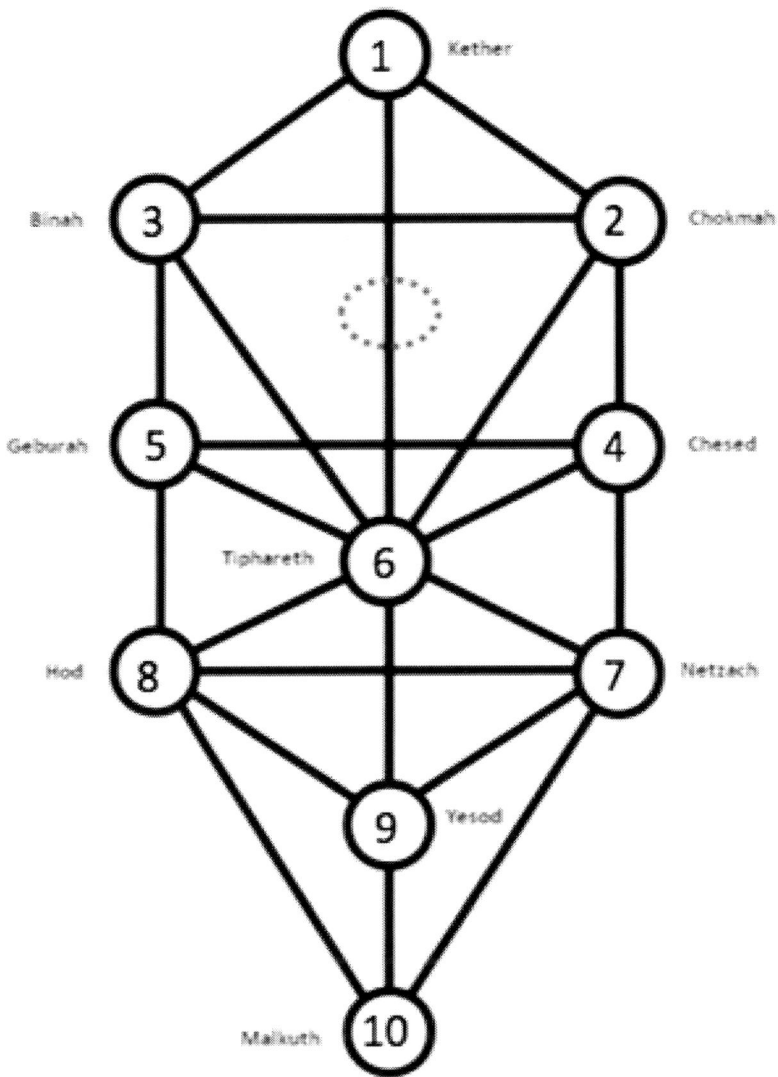

Fig. 1

The Spheres of the Tree of Life

The Path of Evolution

In contrast to the usual place of beginning in the study of the Tree with the First Sphere of Kether and following the Path of Involution, or emanation downward, I have taken the approach of moving upwards on the Tree and beginning our study with the Tenth Sphere of Malkuth. This is the Path of Evolution.

The rationale for this is that we live in the physical world of Malkuth. We are most familiar and comfortable with this landscape and our daily activities allow us to engage directly and concretely with its energy. When we connect with animal life we see the commonalities and disparities of our way of existence, our physiology and group minds. When we tend to and nurture plant life we are stimulating our awareness of those things that are not of our own physical make up, yet serve to feed and heal us; give us oxygen to sustain life and stimulate our senses to a place of beauty and awe. And, when we make use of the mineral kingdom through external means, or by the awareness and acknowledgement of this world as making up the composition of our physical bodies, as well as the planet upon which we thrive, we are again afforded a way of deep and relevant contrast and comparison of those things we intimately know.

Using this information as the foundation upon which we begin ascending the Tree, gives us stable footing and a level of awareness, both of self and our greater world that can support us as we move back in return towards the Divine spark.

Chapter One

MALKUTH

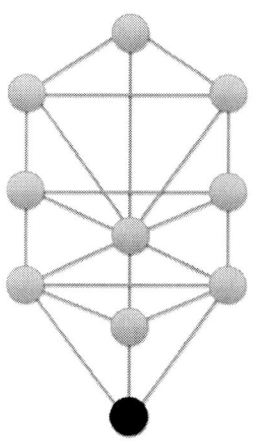

KINGDOM

Dig your fingers deep into the earth
Granules of life and decay
Tiny bits of energy darting here
And there and the smell
Of emerald green moss embedded
Under freshly painted pink nails.

Life force moves down
Submerged appendage and roots beginning
To weave intricate pathways
Towards the heart of the Mother.

Swim deep into the ocean's expanse
Salt and sand the constant companions
Of frothy waves and water filled breath
Fin and tentacle, claw and tooth

Moving, floating, carried by the
Undulating liquid terrain.

Life force moves in spirals and waves
Translucent body glowing in ocean's depths
Settling deep into the sand of floor and
Coiling into renewed matter.

Stone and crystal, cavern and dusted white peak
Architecture of the Gods built from the
Feminine body Divine
Tree home and brush of wing in flight
All scanning the maze of earth below
As sun rises and spills over all of
Living breath and silent decay of return.

Life moves in ascent carried
By the strength of manifest form
Molded in the heated furnace of desire and will
Dome of sky the doorway to the moon's intent.

This is the Kingdom, but what of its ruler
Who holds the place of sovereignty and has
Command over planet's fate?
Flesh and bone and beating of heart
Flowing strength of blood's circuit
Mind of lightning flash and diversity
Embodied in a vessel of form.

And the Great Mother in her wisdom
Holds the Kingdom close to her breast
Heart beat to heart beat the exchange is made
Life is given form and the world of the manifest
Holds the key to the Path of Return.

The Lesson of the Sphere

Keywords

Completion
The Physical Realm
The Place of Life and Death (Beginnings and Endings)

The Energy of the Sphere

The sphere of Malkuth is both in the place of downpour from the realms of higher and more refined energy as well as the place of beginning towards ascension from the grosser, denser form of matter towards a more refined, evolved state of being. This is the sphere of the Elements (earth, air, fire and water) from which all things are formed and is, quite literally, the place of physical manifestation of the creative life force that has emanated down from the spheres above. This is the World of Matter, which is our home during this physical incarnation. Because it is familiar, concrete and ever present there is often the tendency towards not fully recognizing and understanding its subtle qualities and energies. It is similar to the comfortable relationship in which you don't always notice the person in as much detail or with as much appreciation as initially because you now assume you know everything there is to know.

Therefore, the work of this sphere lies in discovering the *Mysteries* of the natural world. This exploration is achieved by establishing a connection with the material world and the alchemical elements comprised within. When we extend our being and consciousness into the "field" of collective consciousness and energetic being, we come to a clearer understanding of the Laws of the Universe and how and by what forces they are governed.

Malkuth is the experience of being fully present in physical form, of connecting with all that makes us truly human and using that as the foundation upon which we rise on the planes to reach our higher consciousness by coming to "know thyself"; and then transferring that knowing into experiencing everything else that comprises this physical world. It is through interaction with and extending our foundations of self in reaching out towards animal, mineral, plant, earth, sky and ocean that we use this wisdom gained as the catalyst towards higher realization and connection.

It is through the five elements that we can begin to build our kingdom on earth and Malkuth is the place where we practice using and expressing more fully those parts of ourselves which although ever present, are not always acknowledged as tools to greater insight. The air we breathe, that fills are lungs and gives alertness to mind and inspiration. The fires that warm us by Sun or inner quickening of desire and will that move us to action. The waters that heal, are contained within our bodies and planet earth, and allow the emotional intuitive self to be birthed. The earth which is our support, our strength and our constant companion as we move through this lifetime of experiences. And, the sacred element of Spirit that is ever present within each living thing, waiting for the work to be done, the connection to be made and the desire towards union to be acted upon. This is the place of Light that illuminates even the shadow self as we ascend on the Tree. These are the keys that unlock the greater mysteries of the Sphere of Malkuth.

Malkuth is the sphere of beginnings and forms the foundation upon which we open to Higher states of consciousness, thereby opening the pathways for a Higher understanding of esoteric knowledge and its application. It is from this place we call "home" that the ascent on the Tree of Life is begun rung by rung and step by step.

The Collective Consciousness

The energy of Malkuth is the work of seeing the interconnectedness of all living things and being active participants in the collective consciousness of the human spirit. When we acknowledge the differences that exist in those things that comprise our world there becomes a point of reference and greater strengthening of our own place within it. We have a clearer understanding of what sets us apart as divine beings having a human experience. We give action to the gifts that we access from both the corporeal and non-corporeal worlds by virtue of our physical nature. And we can offer up our unique and singular contributions towards the evolution of humanity's collective consciousness.

The Glorious Intelligence

Malkuth is considered the Glorious Intelligence. If we consider the reference above regarding Malkuth's state of consciousness as being that of the collective, arriving at a place of Glorious intelligence is an easy conclusion. Intelligence is making use of the mental faculties in a way that is effective and enhances whatever those endeavors are focused upon. The glory that is held in the use of mind is the byproduct of identifying clearly that which is definable and useable. Malkuth has access to this pure intelligence of mind via the *31st Path*. The Hebrew Letter of this path is Shin which means Tooth. When we sink our teeth into a problem and brainstorm to arrive at the best outcome, the result is both Glorious and successful. Sinking our teeth into the task of being at one with the physical nature of our being brings us the Glory of seeing our Divine nature.

The Element of the Sphere
Earth

Malkuth is assigned the element of Earth. Everything about this sphere speaks of the manifest, physical world and all the offerings of its foundational support. Contained within the element of earth are the four kingdoms of animal, plant, mineral and man. Looking at Malkuth from this perspective, we see the collective consciousness that is available and the potential for aligning our physical nature with that of the higher worlds.

Numerical Value

Malkuth is the **Tenth** Sphere on the Tree of Life. The number **10** is the place of restarting the numerical cycles, now doubled, enhanced and amplified by another number at its side. In this case, we have the singular one, the individual **and** the limitless nature of zero, which is both receipt from the All and collaboration with all that has been and will be. It is Matter (1) and Spirit (0) joined in effort. And, after all the work of Malkuth is that of providing the foundation upon which Man, or the singular "I" can aspire towards his omnipresent Divine Nature.

Location on the Tree
Base of Middle Pillar of Equilibrium

Malkuth sits at the base of the Middle Pillar (also known as the Path of Return). This placement puts it in direct relationship to Kether (the Highest point of the Tree) and can be related to **The Law of Correspondence** which is paraphrased thus: *"As above, So below; So below, As above"*. This is the reflection of the Higher Self and the Divine (Kether) looking down upon Its manifest form and the physical being looking upwards and aspiring towards its Face of Divinity.

The Spiritual Experience
Vision of the Holy Guardian Angel

The Holy Guardian Angel is representative of one's truest divine nature. The term is equivalent with the Genius of the Golden Dawn, the Augoeides of Iamblichus, the Atman of Hinduism and the Silent Self of Thelema. The Holy Guardian Angel is not to be confused with the Higher Self. It is outside of and on a higher plane than man in his highest form. It can be likened more to the interface or liaison between man in his Divinity and the Limitless All and it is through knowledge of and subsequent conversation with the Holy Guardian Angel that we form the continual stream of connection with our Higher Selves. In Malkuth, it is this vision and ultimate aspiration that moves us towards the energies of the spheres above. It is this yearning for return to the God Self that sets our foot along the path of greater knowing and moves us beyond the physical limitations perceived.

The Illusion of the Sphere
Materialism

When we become trapped in the desire and quest for accumulation of "things, we amass wealth but this wealth is built upon that which serves no higher purpose. There is also no need to live a life of austerity to reach the place of Spiritual enlightenment. Embracing all that the physical realms have to offer and tempering it with balance by using just what is needed and giving back that which is received in a way that is of benefit to all, as well as honoring your own needs (not wants) holds you in a place of Light where you can more fully be open to the abundance of the Universe without being consumed by the glamour of wanting that which is illusory at best and the heaviest of chains at worst.

The Briatic Color(s)
Black, Citrine, Russet, Olive Green

The Magickal Image
A Young Woman Crowned and Throned

This is Gaia as the maiden. She is ripe and full of the potential of creation, transformation and exploration of self-knowledge. Her crown is that of greenery and bone; of Divine Kingship bestowed as nurturer of the planet and her throne is crafted of mountain and valley the acknowledgement of strength and foundation. This is the living throne that is the verdant and fertile world she rules.

Expression through The Four Worlds

Atziluth- The Creative Urge

Earth/Grain Gods & Goddesses

In the sphere of Malkuth this world is exemplified in the archetypical energy of those Deities who contain both properties of the earth (as in Ceres and grain) and its cycles of life and death. They encompass all that gives life; the quickening of birth, the first spark of creative idea. They are the catalyst, the initiator and the instigator holding all within a mantle of strength and foundation.

Briah - Creation of a Concept - Archangel

Archangel Sandalphon

Awareness of the connection of everyday things to the Divine is the lesson of Briatic Malkuth. The Archangel Sandalphon rules over the atomic structure of the Earth, its domains and all its forms. He also oversees the evolution of all species of life on earth and guides the energies of the angels, the Ischim, in stimulating the urge towards that divine nature. Sandalphon is reflected as Metatron in Kether and as such is thought to be the tallest of the Archangels with feet planted firmly in the Kingdom of Malkuth and head aloft in the realms of Kether. His presence is felt rather than seen and he is the comforting thought or pang of conscience calling us to a place of positive action towards our Higher Selves.

Sandalphon works with Uriel, Archangel of the Earth, who in the realm of Spiritual Earth rules the Elemental Kings and controls the elements themselves. Additionally, Sandalphon is responsible for the vaster more complex structure of the planet itself independent of its life forms.

Yetzirah - Forming the Image of the Concept
Angels - Ischim - The Souls of Fire

The name "Ischim" is the plural form of the words for man (Ish) and woman (Isha) in their evolved states. Striking a match to light a sacred candle is the act of the Element of Fire under the control of the Ischim who are directed by and in the care of Sandalphon. This is the quickening process undergone by the seeker on the path of spiritual evolvement. The place where will and desire take hold to ignite the hunger for movement, change and transformation. These are the fires of a kundalini awakening in Eastern spiritual practice and the ascension of the uraeus in Egyptian alchemy. The Ischim are the sacred fires of the inner hearth, that once the flame has been lit, burn as a beacon of Light eternally.

Assiah - Manifestation
Planet - Earth

Malkuth is the sphere of dominance in this world. Its energy is concerned with direct experience of the Elements (air-fire-water-earth) and awareness of their Ruling Archangels. The elements in this form are not just the physical representation but the deeper esoteric meaning contained within each.

The Elements and their Ruling Archangels

Element	Archangel	Keywords
Air	Raphael	Thought, Mind, Intellect
Fire	Michael	Desire, Will, Transformation
Water	Gabriel	Emotion, Intuition, The Divine Feminine
Earth*	Uriel	Stability, Foundation, Strength-The Sacred Masculine

The plane of manifestation is the place of Man as Divinity (the fifth element of Spirit) whose soul's purpose is to gain mastery over the Elemental Worlds and evolve beyond the confines and limitations of bodies made of cellular material.

* ***Earth*** in this sphere is multilayered in meaning. It is the physical planet upon which we live, the energetic structure of the planet in relationship to the Universe ***and*** the energy of the element of earth as represented by strength, foundation and the building block.

The Living Tree: Personal Study
Earthly Delights

This set of exercises is intended to make you more aware of the elements in their physical form that are ever constant. Try to engage all of your senses: smell, sight, sound, taste, touch and hearing.

Connecting with the Elements:

Rainy Day- Take a walk during a rainy day. Note the feel of the rain on your face and skin. Observe the puddles and the effect the water has on the dirt, grass or pavement.

Out at Noon- On a sunny day, go outside as close to noon as possible. Sit or stand and bask in the sun's light. Take note of the warmth on your skin and the heat on your body. Observe the shadows that are formed when the sun's light is shaded under tree or canopy of cover. How does the richness of light and color fade or intensify?

Windy Day- Go outside on a windy day. Make note of the feel of the wind on your body. The direction and flow of pattern you feel moving against you. How do the trees respond that are around you? Do you notice any weave of pattern as the wind blows across the grass? Do you feel uplifted, as though you could take flight? Or, do you feel as though you are being pressed down upon and held firmly and rooted to the spot?

Earth's Bounty- Select a variety of root vegetables and combine all into a soup or stew. As you wash and prepare each, take a moment to connect with its energy. Visualize its growth and emanation from the planting of a seed. As you sit to eat from the earth's fruits, offer up thanks for the sustaining quality that is our support and foundation.

Chapter Two

YESOD

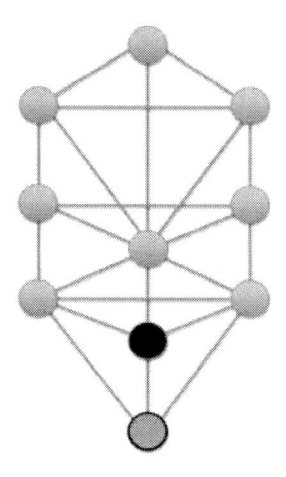

FOUNDATION

Milky whiteness luminescence
Sparkles through veils of dreamtime
Images, shape and form bourne
On gossamer wings of faery flight
And angels beckon from heavenly
Clouds of billowy breath.

Mirror reflects back the beauty of mortal's soul
And yearning feeds the hunger of
Unfulfilled desires and needs
Behind the mask of eternity the
Phantom smiles a gaping grin
And spidery fingers tap out
The rhythm of carnival's retreat
And memories flood the pages
Of dusty shelf-worn books.

While the drone of life story's
Narrative hums and buzzes
Around the hornet's nest
Each stinging more precisely
Each leaving an indelible
Mark as the honey sweetly
Drips from the catacombs
Of Queen Bee's grand design.

Within the sphere of mystery
The moon glows ever bright
And eyes that have no use
For human sight peer
Deeply into the cavernous dark
Moving carefully through the
Storehouse of illusion.

But once the vault is opened
And inspiration comes
Shard-like slicing through
The test has been mastered
The seeker now illumined
And filled with Luna's grace
Moves boldly and sure footed.

The mind has been set free
Fragile fingers reach ever upward
And the heart waits patiently
Behind the reflection of
The closed door.

The Lesson of the Sphere

Keywords

Illusion
Thought Forms
Dream World
Memory

The Energy of the Sphere

In Hebrew, the word Yesod means "foundation" and the "sod" portion alone means "mystery". This should give clue as to the energies of the qabalistic sphere of Yesod. It is the stuff of dreams, fantasies, memory and the dwelling place of true magick. This sphere holds the key to the unknown and the unknowable. Just as matter itself resides in Malkuth, the focus and energy which make it "living matter" is contained within the essence of Yesod. As we descend from the higher spheres and move through the varied energies of each of the preceding we come to rest in Yesod, the beginning phase of creation of a thoughtform; the storehouse of images only, without the benefit of the life energy needed before these images can move into a state of manifestation in Malkuth.

Yesod is known as the "Treasure House of Symbols". It is here that the Akashic records, which are said to contain the memory and experiences of every living being are held within the substance of Aether (spirit). This attribute alone can give rise to illusion, false conceptions and a deluded sense of Soul's purpose. It is a world of shadow and illusion; being held in a state of "in-between". It is higher than the physical plane of Malkuth, yet lower than the Divine/spiritual plane that would provide the necessary discernment to determine that which is illusory in nature and that which is a true expression of reality. By virtue of this state of mediation and filter the function of Yesod provides informed access to the Astral which contains the necessary accumulation of symbols and images that can be further classified, processed, filtered and assimilated to allow movement to the higher realms. In ascent up the Tree these images and collected information come from the place of the concrete manifest energy of Malkuth and human experience. And, in downpour those pure ideas and mental processes of Higher Mind co-mingle with what is reaching upwards. Yesod is the place of allegory and allusion to things of a higher nature. Because the information is often muddled or distorted (as in the fun house mirror) it becomes necessary to strengthen the emotion of Trust. Trusting that the information being revealed is the truth emanating from a pure source, and trusting that you will be able to learn the appropriate lesson of the allegory.

Yesod is notably the sphere of the moon. And, just as the physical moon of our world goes through its tides and cyclical changes and has great effect on our physical earth; this principle is also true of the interaction between Yesod and Malkuth. The Moon was man's first timekeeper and generated awareness of the seasons, the water's ebb and flow, evolution and change. It also gave light to the awareness of the cyclic nature of life and the natural surroundings. On the Tree, moving through the energies of Yesod is to move in accord with the **Cosmic Law of Rhythm**; the natural cyclic nature of all things and the evolution and transformation at the level of the Soul through these waters of higher life.

Yesod resonates to the sacral chakra and as such is the plane of sexuality and the potential underlying each act of coupling. It is the fertile breeding ground for all future spiritual development as you move upwards through the Tree. Its nature is that of fecundity and quickening. **By definition, fecundity is:**

1. The ability to produce offspring, especially in large numbers.

2. The ability to produce many different and original ideas.

This energy is beyond simply being fertile. In Malkuth we were matter incarnate. In Yesod we become matter quickened by greater substance and spirit. We become the replication of all parts of self; each having the ability for quickening and enlivening; and thus become co-creators.

Yesod is the psychological equivalent of the subconscious and through dream work and cultivating a state of emotional health and well-being, its energies reveal the greater work of the astral and inner planes in preparation for rising on the planes and experiencing the energies of the Higher Realm spheres. The process of self-awareness is begun in the sphere of Yesod, and the shadow world of the Astral is the symbolic underworld of the subconscious. This is where work is done around personal phantoms and the shadow self is encountered, assimilated and recognized as the Illusory Self. The embracing and acceptance of this shadow or darker part of self is the necessary component for union of all parts of self and gaining mastery over this aspect gives strength to that part of the being that stands in the place of the light. This is the basic role of polarity in action. Light and dark, higher and lower all working in accord with the other and having awareness of the dynamics of each.

Yesod is the great initiator and to come to an understanding of its nature is to have progressed through an initiatory process of death and rebirth; moving from the mundane realm (Malkuth) and having passed successfully through the shadows and mystery of the astral to heightened awareness. Through this process, the capacity for intuitive insight and a quickening of the Divine life force within is the final result of the synthesis of all the accumulated information gained from the symbols and images presented at the Yesodic plane.

The Informed Consciousness

The energy of Yesod is one of Consciousness that is informed and working in accord creatively with that information received. The imagery and access to collective memory, thought and action serves to enhance the energy of Yesod and bring the seeker to a place of having the discernment needed to sort through what is presented. The dream state is one of the places where this action of discernment is played out. What is gathered in this state of dream awareness serves to inform the actions that are taken in waking consciousness; even at times when there is no memory of what was received. This is the pure nature of a consciousness that has achieved a state of communication and trust with the Higher Self. This is the place of a consciousness that is in a constant state of dialogue with that which informs the Universe.

The Pure Intelligence

Yesod is known as Pure Intelligence. It stands as the receptacle of downpour from Hod, the sphere of pure mind and having received thought devoid of censoring, testing and analysis, Yesod serves to provide the necessary checks and balances. It works upon the sorting and reshaping of what will pass through the filter of unbiased judgment. It purifies and clarifies through its initiatory energy and transforms what passes through either to make fit for the ascent to higher realms or the descent into physical matter.

The Element of the Sphere

Air

Yesod is assigned the element of Air and the ephemeral experience of sensing what surrounds you, yet being unsure of where it has originated and where it is going. You are simply caught in the airiness of its path. Much like the breezy day, that begins with gentle caresses, then moves into a frenzied state of blustery conditions and finally quiets back to a state of calm. Opening the flood gates of memory stimulated by the subconscious and collective unconscious can often leave the dreamer in a state of feeling as though they just weathered a potent storm.

Numerical Value

Yesod is the **Ninth** Sphere and it is interesting to note that in the Major Arcana of the Tarot the card attributed to the number **9** is The Hermit. The Hermit is the seeker on the path who turns within in search of the inner light. Removing himself from the mundane needs of the physical (Malkuth) world and gaining the necessary insight to provide the quickening of the Higher Self in a place of mystery, darkness and seclusion. In numerology, the number nine relates to death and rebirth, acting as the gate of movement into a new state of being. And, it is in this state of self-awareness, inner light and true wisdom that we are made ready to ascend back to the place of the Source of All, the sphere Kether.

Location on the Tree

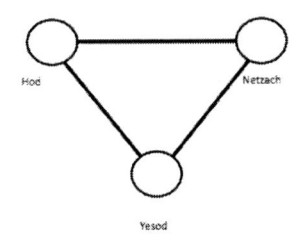

Fig. 10

Yesod sits at the base of the Astral/Lunar Triangle. On the ascent up the Tree this is the first place of co-joined effort. The place that holds dominion over the fueling of the energetic triad of fire and transformation. The state of positive, negative and neutrality working in harmony as the energy rises towards the higher vibrations of the upper spheres of emanation. On the descent from the place of Kether and its subsequent emanations, Yesod becomes the Divine receptacle that filters, refines, remolds and provides the finishing touches before the word, the thought and the creative urge become manifest. It is also the first sphere that connects the first set of the outer paths of the Tree. It is the unifier and middle point of balance before the designation and split into the pillars of Mercy and Might; Force and Form.

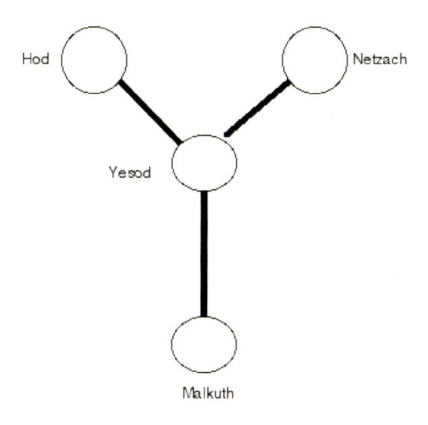

Fig. 11

Yesod is also placed at the Apex of the point of the triangle before the descent into matter. Conversely it is also the point of the first triangle of spheric energy encountered on journey towards the Godhead of Kether. Its position serves as a gateway separating our physical being before it is filtered through the Astral to emerge within the Higher Realms of understanding or Pure Intelligence.

There is a constant interchange and balance extending from the consciousness of Malkuth into the subconscious; that energy first encountered in Yesod on the ascent upwards in movement towards the unconsciousness of Yesod at Higher spectrum just before entering into Hod. At a conscious level we live in Malkuth. Within the subconscious we find the answers in the higher aspect of Yesod in its state as Refined Intelligence.

The Yin/Yang of Malkuth and Yesod

| Downpour From
Yesod to Malkuth
Descending | Aspiring Upwards From
Malkuth to Yesod
Ascending |

The dynamics of energy between Malkuth and Yesod could be likened to that of the Yin/Yang. Yesod acts in providing Divine communication and as an interface between gross matter and the realm of the unknowable. Its work is in moving man beyond the constraints of physical being towards the Divine Source. Once having learned the lessons of the Akashic records and the Inner workings of the Astral Plane the polarities merge and blend as One.

The Spiritual Experience
Vision of the Machinery of the Universe

The wheel of time turns and the cogs are maintained and well oiled to ensure there is no cessation of this mighty endeavor. It is the inner workings of all that exists in the past, present and future. All are entwined within the memory and temple of creative flow. This is our independence based on what we already know to be true at a manifest level, which is then filtered, modified, and adapted by the illusion of Yesod which prompts a closer look. Yesod acts to hold together the form; thus enmeshing the denser particles of matter that create the physical realm. This is one of the principles of Quantum Physics and the theory of the Field.

The Illusion of the Sphere
Delusion

We move through the world intent upon our course and create and construct truisms and beliefs that are often, when more closely examined, not of our creation at all. Yet we cling steadfastly and with strength and conviction to the declaration that these are indeed our truths. We choose to remain in a dream state because this absolves us from the consequences that our awakened choices may have. Spending some time cultivating the imagination is a pleasurable and rewarding pursuit, but allowing the illusion of what is merely imagination to replace or consume what is viable food for creative outpour is the folly of Yesod. To remain in the place of dreams is to be veiled forever.

The Briatic Color
Violet

The Briatic Color of Yesod is Violet. Violet is a combination of reds and blues, each of a softer scale and more cool intensity than that of purple. If we think of the energies of Yesod, it is this cool tone that prevails in its workings. A certain cool detachment that allows for the flow of dreams and information to flow without the intensity of over-coloring or over-saturating the input with too much intensity of will (Red) or the overwhelming need to heal (Blue) what is being presented. It is the blending of the subtleties of both.

The Magickal Image
A Beautiful Naked Man, Very Strong

One could think of Atlas in this imagery. The beauty lay in the seamless union of man and world. Yesod works to support the weight of the upper spheres of the Tree in much the same way. All being dependent on its strength to allow what transpires in the heavenly worlds above to be held just beyond the actual grasp of mankind until he has proven his determination and effort towards reaching those lofty aims.

Expression Through The Four Worlds

Atziluth - The Creative Urge

**The Supreme Lord of Life
Fertility Gods and Lunar Goddesses
All Deities of Triple Aspect**

Within the sphere of Yesod, Atziluth is exemplified in the archetypical energy of those Deities who provide the fertile ground for inspiration, imagination and who are ultimately the catalyst for higher thought (at the level of Hod). The goddesses of the Moon enhance the inner and intuitive sight and allow the flow of emotions in accord with the ebb and flow of the tides. The triple aspects of Maiden-Mother-Crone or Youth-Father-Sage show the ability for change and transition moving from one stage of being and level of experience to another with each dependent upon the knowledge and memory of the other to give the necessary clarity of the experience of the previous stage.

Within the realm of Atziluth, this creative urge is brought forth as life begets life through the Yesodian process of discernment, flow of increase and decrease and through the filter of the emanations from the other spheres on the Middle Pillar (through equilibrium).

Briah - Creation of a Concept - Archangel
Gabriel - Water - The Divine Messenger Bearing a Trumpet

Maintaining a sense of order based on truth and reality is the lesson of Briatic Yesod. The Archangel Gabriel is one of Truth. The trumpet in earlier times was not of metal but was seen as a symbol of fertility or the horn of plenty and was considered phallic in nature bearing the seed of potential. There is the allusion to sexual potency and virility around this concept and the place of being the Divine Messenger, then becomes the messenger of that which is yet to be realized, that which is yet to be born and made viable. The association with water is the reference to the waters of creation, the vehicle and conductor of the electrical spark or charge which animates and gives life to whatever is the receptacle of that energy. Gabriel is one of the four Archangels, each of whom are assigned an element. Gabriel is guardian of the West and the waters that flow. Thus, the association with the lunar tides and birthing waters.

Yetzirah - Forming the Image of the Concept
Angels - Kerubim - Strength

Just as Malkuth was the sphere of dominance in the manifest world of Assiah, Yesod is the preeminent sphere in the Yetziratic world. This is the place of designing the template or image for what will later become manifest reality.

In this domain, the Kerubim, or angels associated with Strength are the needed force and energy to move those from the inertia of idle dreaming to a place of higher thought (HOD) and finally manifest creation (Malkuth). In the ascent up the Tree the Kerubim use the catalytic energy of the Ischim - The Souls of Fire- that have done the necessary work in Malkuth to ensure movement and bolster it with the energy of resolve towards completion. The recurring theme of strength within this sphere is the key to its greatest mystery, for the Kerubim are the formators of energy directed towards the goal of creation and manifestation of what has been created.

Assiah - Levanah (The Moon)

What are the images that come to mind when you think of the moon, its energy and its cycles. It is under the watchful eye of the moon that we sleep and enter the state of dreamtime and unconscious thought is given form through our subconscious reality. It is also upon Malkuth (or Earth) that the radiance of the moon is apparent; shifting throughout its cycles of being unseen, waxing full bright and then waning back into the unseen. This is the compelling energy of Yesod in its place within the Assiac realm. This is the cycle of memory and imagery, moving through its place of unseen potential, then waxing with enthusiasm towards climatic product and finally returning once again to the place of transformed energy that has yet to be actualized.

The name "Levanah" is the phonetic form of the Hebrew word for moon and means "lunar beam". It is the constancy of the Levanah (or lunar beam) that pours down upon those of manifest being that brings them to a state of rising on those beams towards a place of higher consciousness recalling the memory of their Divine nature.

The Living Tree: Personal Study
The Moon of Day Light

This set of exercises is intended to make you more aware of the impact of dreams, the imagination and develop discernment of what is reality and what is illusory in nature. When we move deeper into our own inner worlds and explore the many and varied forms that thought takes when fueled by the emotional and intuitive self we move closer towards mastery of making manifest the Divine beings we inherently are. Although imagination is usually easily stirred in most, refining and molding it into a useful tool takes practice and work. Similarly, being able to remember the pattern and content of our dreams and/or moving into a state of lucid dreaming is the key to unlocking the mysteries and secretes of the subconscious and unconscious mind.

Dream Time

Day dreams are often useful tools for strengthening the powers of visualization and attracting positive results into your life. Allow yourself 30-minutes of uninterrupted time. As you sit quietly, let your imagination flow as you contemplate a new job, a new way of doing something, a new activity or anything that you have stored away in your memory as simply wishful thinking. Allow the situation to unfold and add as much detail as you wish. Try to engage all of your senses in this waking dream. After you have built these images up, consciously and with intent, acknowledge that the imagery will be recalled when you wish and in as much detail as you have experienced. Each time you revisit this scenario try to give more detail and clarity to the experience.

Chapter Three

HOD

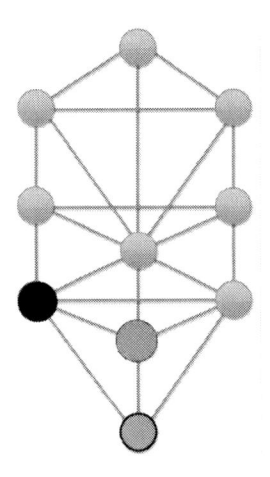

GLORY

Scintillating mind of reason and intellect
Whose course is drawn from
The halls of libraries' tomes.
Echoes of the One emanate down
Into the hollow of conductivity.

The blueprint of electric charge and
Inspiration's whim creating the
Alchemical tube to hold the elixir of
Manifest form.

Teachings and truths spun together
And finally issued forth
Flow on the currents of communication
And Hermes sets in stone the power
Of mind and word.

The precision of the surgeon's scalpel has
Cut away the extraneous matter and
Sun's grace has heated the water's core
Love has poured honey to soothe the
Gaping wounds and bridge the chasm of
Beating heart and labyrinth of mind.

Luna's mirror has sent the message of
Return or receipt of ideology finely tuned
And in finality the most pure form of clarity
Seeps down to ocean's edge
Granules of sandy time dense with
Outpour from horizon's great beyond.

Scintillating Mind of Reason and Intellect
The seed of Thought receives the food of the Gods
And once again blooms anew.

The Lesson of the Sphere

Keywords

Mind
Thought
Invention
Science
Logic

The Energy of the Sphere

Hod is the sphere of Pure Reason and Logic that has not received the cross flow and balance of heart and emotion (Netzach). Its function is to make Order of the Universe through objective reasoning and higher thought.

The Sphere of Communication

The Planetary ruler of Hod is Mercury, so it is fitting that this sphere is considered the sphere of communication. Within its rationale and reasoning are the tools that may be used in discovering the deeper mystery contained within information. It is through the crystal clarity of pristine thinking that enables a better and more efficient means of communicating what knowledge has been extracted. It is also this modality that makes Hod the ideal energetic support for ritual work. Effective ritual and devotional practice are honed from clear and purposeful intent. If that intent is not objectively informed the resulting product of that ritual will not be as strong or as durable in form and focus. If, however, objective thought and clear Higher Mind is working in accord with focused intent, the results become the inroads and precursors to future successful magick, devotional or spiritual practice.

Magickal work is of no value if there is no Understanding (BINAH) of its logical order, structure and form (HOD) gained through dissection, sacrifice, and excision (GEBURAH) of all that is extraneous and illusory (YESOD)

The Water Temple

The Sphere of Hod is also known as The Water Temple. This refers to the connection of the lower triad spheres of Hod, Netzach and Yesod. It is within this Temple that the emotional and the intellectual combine to become something greater than the singularity of each. It is the quality of mind and reason reflecting back to itself that the clarity of pure thought is generated. This is also the place of reflecting the truth of the Higher Mind. In truth, one could think of this as the temple of birthing waters that carry the breath of mind having been catalyzed by the transformative Gates of Yesod.

The Awakened Consciousness

The energy of Hod is one of Awakened Consciousness. Being able to detach itself from constriction and limitation of pure emotional consideration allows Hod to respond in a way that is both liberating and unencumbered. This light of pure thought illumines each action and this conscious fully awakened state of awareness is no longer held captive by the dream state of Yesod. It is consciousness that acts and reacts in accord with the natural laws of mental process; pure brilliance emanating from a state of pure being that is fully awakened to the possible outcomes of every endeavor and being able to clearly and vibrantly allow these solutions to move in fluid uninterrupted stream.

The Absolute Intelligence

Hod is known as the Absolute Intelligence. **By definition:**

Absolute: The one ultimate reality that does not depend on anything, and is not relative to anything else.
and
Intelligence: An entity capable of rational thought, especially one that does not have a physical form.

This form of Intelligence is Absolute because it originates in the upper spheres of Binah and Chokmah, receiving the Mercy and Grace of Chesed in downward emanation. Its mind is not quantifiable by any set of standards and it has not yet reached into the denser realms that have been filtered through the lens of Yesod. Just as matter itself resides in Malkuth, the focus and energy which make it "living matter" is contained within the essence of Yesod. As we ascend towards Hod, we reach the place where the first "idea" of that matter is born. Hod is the drafting board that goes through each step carefully and objectively in the planning stages before it receives the energizing quickening at the level of Yesod. Hod decodes and analyzes but, it also reveals deceptions and untruths.

The Element of the Sphere
Water

Hod is assigned the element of Water. This water is typified as the flow of mind in constant and continual movement. It is the constant stream of download that runs a pure and unspoiled course with the singular goal of informing whatever is in receipt of its inspiration. Some of this channel will be collected and brought further down into the filters that will determine final manifestation, but most will remain in constant movement of flow until one droplet of viable potential ripples outward in its effect.

Numerical Value

Hod is the **Eighth** Sphere. Within the energy of the number **8** is great power and the sacrifice of contraction and expansion. The holding and funneling of what wishes to expand and then the ultimate release into a great circle of expansive formlessness. It is also the doubling of the stability and foundation expressed by the number four. It is the mirroring of two bases of four sides that reflect back to one another in perfect symmetry. The union of Higher and Lower Mind, the duality and polarity of pairs that have been elevated upon a strong and durable foundation.

Hod is the Sphere of Transmutation

The essence and spark of potential for creative thought lay within its depths and what emerges is the mind touch of the Higher transmuted for downpour into manifest form. **Transmutation is defined thusly:**

1. Change: A change, or the process of change.

2. In Physics: The change of one element into another: the transformation of the atom of one chemical element into the atom of another by disintegration or nuclear bombardment (the work of Geburah in moving down the Pillar of Severity into Hod).

Location on the Tree
Base of Pillar of Severity

Hod enjoys the auspicious location of sitting at the base of the Pillar of Severity (Form). It receives the downpour from Geburah (Might through transformative excision) and Binah (The Great Mother of Understanding). It is the Ending place of Divine Thought that has been finely honed and created through emanation from the Higher Spheres. Hod is the Seat of Consciousness of Form.

Awareness- Higher Intuition	Binah Understanding	Vision of Sorrow
Consciousness- Will	Geburah Severity	Vision of Power
Linear Thought- Reason	Hod Glory	Vision of Splendor

Pillar of Severity

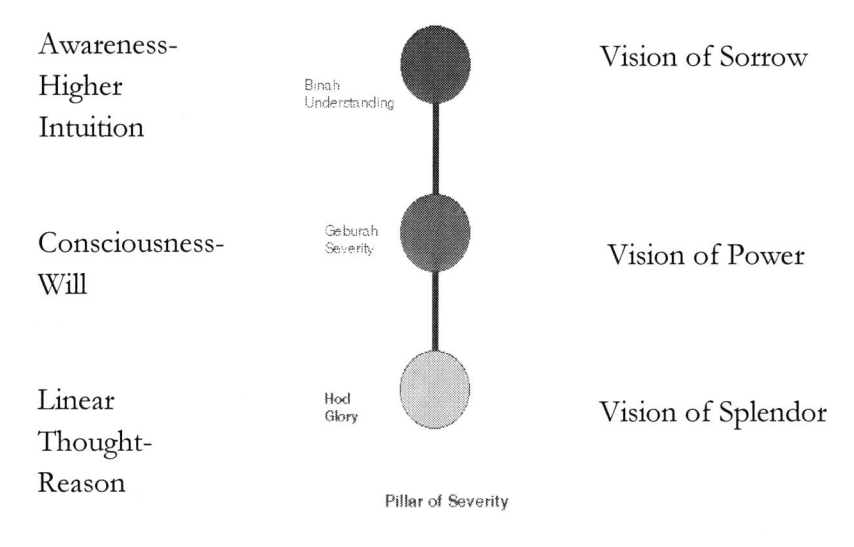

Fig. 12

It is the place of all manner of inspiration inclusive of science, the written word, music, art, and language. Thus, in the continued descent from Hod into Yesod the illusions of Yesod are the filtered forms of Divine Inspiration. At the level of Yesod, this may take the form of difficulty with interpretation of the symbols and images that are presented. Awareness and Higher Intuition, when brought down to the place of Consciousness, join to stimulate the will to create at the level of the Mind. As this will moves into the waters of Hod, the Fire of Will directed through a Divine All-knowingness moves through those currents of mind activity and generates a circuit of electrical charge that becomes the ohm or watt of energy that moves along the circuit board of linear thought and reason.

Capacity of the Mind

Hod is the first sphere on the ascent of the Tree that has multiple paths of connection including the place of sitting at the base of the Pillar of Severity. It is also connected via Paths to Tiphareth (the central sphere of the Tree); to the right to Netzach (the base sphere of the Pillar of Mercy) and to one reaching upwards out of the moon sphere of Yesod. Just as the mind and brain have many chambers, corridors and paths contained within, Hod offers many routes of emanation from its core to be opened and awakened. As the place of structure, order, categorization, analysis and making sense of it all, Hod also serves as the distributor of the work that has been accomplished in Malkuth and Yesod upwards towards the more refined spheres.

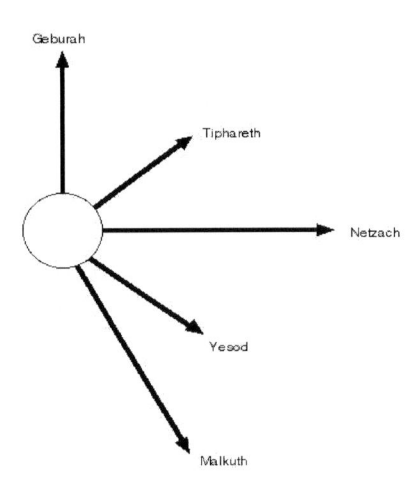

Fig. 13

The Spiritual Experience
Vision of Splendor

In the sphere of Hod the vision of splendor is one of splendor of the workings and order within the Universe. Intuitive thought has been brought to the place of intellectual understanding of these inner workings. Knowledge of how and why things proceed the way in which they do and how the energies of ebb and flow of the natural rhythms and cycles of the Universe intellectually make sense. **By definition, Splendor is:**

Something that is impressive, magnificent or brilliant.

It is this exact vision that opens the greater mind to a truth of the place of each being and energy in the vastness of an organized, logical and unified whole.

The Illusion of the Sphere
Falsehood, Dishonesty

The Illusion of Hod is false ego based on faulty knowledge. It is the allowance of what is subjective, personality biased information to fill the coffers of our minds as being the stuff of unbiased thought. Furthermore, claiming credit for those brilliant seeds of inspiration when they are nothing more than the over inflated toutings of one craving acknowledgement for being wise, breeds the dishonesty of validation that is not merit based, nor is it sound in it reasoning.

As the time honored thought on this matter goes, true wisdom cannot be found within the knowledge of book learning and course study. True wisdom is the result of experience at the level of connection to a Higher Consciousness and taking what has been learned through books and study and transforming it into an enlivened part of oneself that cannot be disputed, argued, reasoned away or often even explained to others who have not also had similar experience on the path towards Wisdom.

The Briatic Color
Orange

Now that we've moved up the Tree through the spheres of Malkuth, Yesod and Hod let's take a look at the color attributions of the spheres through the Four Worlds. There is an interesting pattern and cross relationship that supports the knowledge that the Tree occurs simultaneously in multiple replications of itself within each of the spheres.

	Malkuth	**Yesod**	**Hod**
Atziluth	Yellow	Indigo	Violet Purple
Yetzirah	Russet, Black Citrine and Olive	Violet	Russet Red
Briah	Black, Russet, Citrine and Olive flecked Gold	Very Dark Purple	Orange
Assiah	Black, with rays of Olive and Yellow	Citrine flecked with Azure	Yellowish Brown flecked with Gold

The Magickal Image
A Hermaphrodite

The Hermaphrodite as magickal symbol for Hod contains the potential for self-creation and is at once both and separate. It is from this view point that the mechanism of reason and thought manifest. In order to exist, there is the necessary condition of union between what is like itself and what is the complimentary pair, yet different from itself.

The mythic tale of Hermaphroditus gives metaphoric insight to the combined energies of Netzach (Aphrodite) and Hod (Hermes) or Heart and Mind. The progeny of this union is that which is most desired (Will). The Nyads are female water nymphs and here we have the vehicle of water that will serve as the transformative agent. It is the flow of the feminine that has been fired with the desire for the product of unified heart and mind. With this awareness of the Divine the energy merges and blends to produce that which is self-creating and self-illuminating.

Hermaphroditus' name is derived from those of his parents Hermes and Aphrodite. According to legend, Hermaphroditus was raised by nymphs on Mount Ida, a sacred mountain in Phrygia (present day Turkey). At the age of fifteen, he grew bored of his surroundings and traveled the cities of Lycia and Caria. It was in the woods of Caria, that he encountered Salmacis the Nyad in her pool. She was overcome by lust for the boy, and tried to seduce him, but was rejected. When he thought she was gone, Hermaphroditus undressed and entered the waters of the empty pool. Salmacis sprang out from behind a tree and jumped into the pool. She wrapped herself around him, kissing him and caressing his body. While he struggled, she called out to the gods asking that they never part from one another. Her wish was granted, and their bodies blended into one hermaphrodite form

This idea of containing both yet being one is also found in idea of thinking in pairs. Another fitting symbol for Hod would be the Caduseus; twin, yet polarized basili or serpents entwined on a central staff (the Middle Pillar). Each serpent crossing, intersecting and drawing upwards with it the information contained and germinated at each intersecting point. Until, finally reaching the uppermost point (Kether) the two become the One of Divine inspiration that is both Imminent Thought and the Singular Mind.

Expression Through The Four Worlds

Atziluth - The Creative Urge
The Supreme Lord of Life
Deity of Thought - Learning - Knowledge - Communication

Egyptian: Toth- Lord of Learning and Keeper of Records
Greek: Hermes- the Messenger of the Gods (Binah/Chokmah)
Roman: The God Mercury

Within the sphere of Hod, the world of Atziluth is exemplified in the archetypical energy of those Deities who provide the essence of thought and idea in its most pure and abstract sense. Moreover, these bursts of inspiration and clarity of idea are deftly brought to a place of communication. This is represented in the energies of the God Hermes whose task it was to bring the information received from the Gods (Binah and Chokmah) down into the realms of pure idea (Hod). This modality of knowledge is held within the container of true wisdom or the concept of an idea in its most primal form before the filtering and enhancement of emotion, personality and the density of manifest form. The trickster nature of this God is one to be aware of. Manipulation and cunning are the mind stuff of those wishing to present the persona of all knowing, and many have been fooled out of money, livelihood and more when the misuse of thought and idea was bandied about.

As exemplified by the Egyptian God Toth, this process of mind is not limited by any basis of expertise. He is at once master, creator, co-creator and keeper of all knowledge that was, is and will be. In this sense the Creative Urge (Atziluth) is simultaneously occurring within the realm of Higher mind in a constant downpour or emanation from the Divine Source of the All-Knowing.

Briah - Creation of a Concept- Archangel
Archangel Michael

Transmuting thought to a higher form is the work of Hod through the catalytic Fires of the Archangel Michael. Michael is associated with Fire and is considered the Watcher and the Guardian. The work of Fire is to purge and transform those things it imposes its will upon. It is through this means that the primal ideas and pure intellect that is devoid of emotional component and refinement (Netzach) is made ready to move down in emanation to Yesod for further filtering and rendering. In its form upwards on the Pillar of severity this "firing in the kilns" serves to burn away the dross in preparation for final excision through the energies of Geburah. Michael is the defender in times of imbalance and as such he wields the might of his sword in the flash of light to bring clarity to this state of pure reason before it moves to a place of heart and healing in Netzach.

Yetzirah - Forming the Image of the Concept
Angels - Beni Elohim - Children of the Gods

Children follow in the footsteps of their parents, and in this case, we, as the children of Binah and Chokmah have the ability to create through the energy of HOD a world of our own making. In the purely manifest aspect this becomes the physical birth and creation of children, as well as a more limited ability to create and manifest spiritual thoughtforms. All of these "children", however, are the result of the polarizing effects of the union of male and female energy constructs. These are Divine thoughtforms, born of polarized Divine consciousness that have come down to a place of being more readily available to the expanded human consciousness. These are the rays of inspiration that are ever so fleeting, the proverbial "light bulb" moments when the ideas and inspirations come rushing in at lightning speed from a source we can clearly define as being "more than" our own range of experience. And those that can pass through the illusions and trials of Yesod are those that come into the place of the Manifest Children (thoughts) of the Gods.

Assiah - The World of Expression - Planetary Mercury

Mercury is the realm of all manner of communication. In the sphere of Hod, this is communication of and through a Higher Mind touch, emanating downward and potentially coming to a place of concrete idea and thought in the manifest physical world. The caution here, however, is one of miscommunication. When communication moves into the domains of pure intellect, logic can often take the place of pure reason. We rationalize this or that to be so. We use logic as our defense for choosing one over the other. But pure and Absolute Intelligence is that which has not been directly affected by emotion. This is intellect that is objective and knows nothing other than its own pure state of being which is pure natural mind.

In the Assiatic World, Hod is the union of Higher and Lower Mind. Each serving the other, and each in perfect dialogue with the other. It is the expression of pure intellect brought into the manifest realm and the abstract form becoming the concrete form of physical expression.

The Living Tree: Personal Study

Opening to the Thinking Self

This set of exercises is intended to make you more aware of the impact of your thoughts; where and how they arise and how they can be used as effective tools towards self-knowledge, growth and dialogue with all parts of our spiritual and human natures.

Active Engagement

As you move through your day, take a few minutes in the morning, at lunchtime and before bed to check in with your thinking self. Try to be aware of where some of these perceptions and thoughts have originated. Were they the products of interaction with others?

Were they the products of you sitting quietly and mindfully "brainstorming" the solution to a problem? Were they the products of inspired reading or did they seem to flow from the muses themselves? Although we use the faculty of thought regularly throughout the day, the quality and receptivity of that process are often the results of being on auto-pilot, without much attention to what is actually happening. Try to set aside some time each day (15-minutes is a good starting point) to sit quietly and be fully engaged in what thoughts, ideas and inspirations are moving through you. Write down these ideas. They are often the seeds of a truly inspired idea or even potential answers to something that at a subconscious level may have been of concern. By establishing a routine time to simply "be" with your thoughts, you are facilitating a greater opening to the Universal and Cosmic ideology that surrounds us. And, once that connection is made, you are then opening to the Divine.

Chapter Four

NETZACH

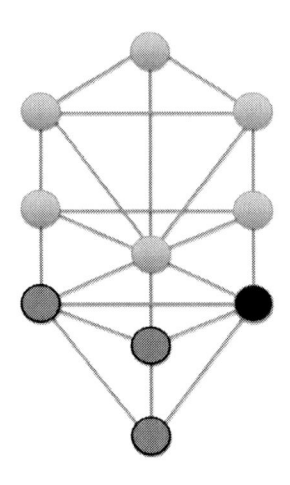

VICTORY

Deep within the heart
Of the emerald jewel
Lay the great mysteries
Of time and love.

The lamp is lit
And glows within
Edges sharp where
Line and point
Intersect poignantly
At the place of equilibrium.

From the wellspring rises
Form of beauty and
Intelligence refined
As Pleiades dance

In response to the
Sound of planets'
Symphony.

And, all is held gently
Contained in beauty's grace
As she unites with clarity of
Mind and focus of heart
Birthing the perfected one
Whose glory mirrors
The sun's radiance
From above.

The Lesson of the Sphere

Keywords

Creativity
Achievement
Synthesis
Union

The Energy of the Sphere
The Illumination of The Self

The sphere of Netzach is the place of establishing the balance of hedonistic and aesthetic ideals. Love is the primary focus, but not at the expense of over indulgence in physical pleasure. This is also the place of expression of Love of Nature in all of her forms. The connection between beauty and the energies that are contained within the force of Nature is a strong one. Even in the Natural world's more disruptive expression, the order and intelligence in design applied in her shaking free from her mantle those disruptions of energy is done with a sense of order, intent and aestheticism.

Netzach is known as the sphere of Victory. The principle of victory here is not one of wanton take-over and infringement of another's space, but rather victory that is found within the triumph over obstacles, whether perceived or real. This over coming is brought to a place of clarity and scrutiny primarily through the action of revealing the true nature of the experience. The resulting balance that occurs is the interaction between Hod and Netzach, academia and pleasure, science and art. This is the work of a polarizing effect. The balance of male and female principles, expansion and contraction, mercy and severity of nature are those obstacles which when brought to a place of control and exertion of will form the basis of foundation for creative outpour.

The Consciousness of Self

The energy of Netzach is one of Consciousness that has come to a place of awareness of its own inherent nature or state of being. Balance or living the place of the middle way can only be achieved when we acknowledge the areas where we over indulge and those areas where effort is lacking. To formulate this discernment requires being fully apprised of our own basic nature. Once this has been established the necessary fine tuning, balancing and bringing to a state of equilibrium can occur. Netzach is the sphere of love, beauty and refinement. It is through the process of refining the parts of self that we can finally acknowledge and truly love the beauty of the resultant outcome. And, that conscious awareness of the newly found self is our place of greatest Victory.

The Occult Intelligence

Netzach is known as the "Occult Intelligence". **By definition Occult means:**

1. Beyond the realm of human comprehension; inscrutable.

The revelations that occur within the sphere of Netzach are those that surpass our human experience. They are the stuff of dialogue between our heart of compassion (Netzach) and our Higher Mind (Hod).

2. Hidden from view or concealed.

Although Netzach provides illumination that allows the Mind stream of Hod to come to its pure insights of intellect infused with emotion, this energy is one that is more subtle and complex in nature.

We could think of this in terms of Netzach's interaction with the pure reason, intellect and inspiration that is the energy of its connecting sphere of Hod. The highest thoughts and loftiest aims are nothing that will ever come to fruition unless there is the spark of radiant light; so pure and refined in its essence that it is the expression of beauty that is incomprehensible at a physical state of being. This radiance alone is also not quite enough to fully catalyze the pure mind stream, there must also be the refined mind touch of the Divine (emanated downwards from the spheres above) similar to the pinnacle of the "Fool" of Tarot's attribute of utter belief and faith that all will be well as he steps forward into the unknown.

The Intelligence of the Heart

Intelligence of the Heart refers to the concept that was explored by scientist and metaphysician, R.A Schwaller DeLubicz during his studies of Egyptian spiritual and alchemical practices. For most, the concept of intelligence is confined to the physiology of the mind and those senses that the mind effects. To the ancient Egyptians, the "heart" was the holder of these attributes of intelligence and deep gnosis.

This way of thinking is deeply reflective of the principles of heart centered Netzach and its force of impact upon Hod, the rational mind. Without this innate intelligence that serves to provide the deeper understanding (realized through expansion and issuance of those qualities of Divine Love) pure reason will never have the necessary glue to produce thoughts of substance and viability. They will always remain within the world of ephemeral and lofty ideals that never come to full fruition.

The Element of the Sphere
Fire

Netzach is assigned the element of Fire. Within the energy of Netzach we can identity this Fire as that of longing, desire and the impetus that coerces the creative urge towards manifestation. The nature of this Fire is to quicken and then spread and reach towards distribution through the flowing waters of Hod. This is the Fire that initially burns very hot and very bright but if not tended carefully will spread out of control and consume that which created it.

Numerical Value

Netzach is the **Seventh** Sphere. Within the energy of the number **7** lay the many paths of higher expression and development. Seven is the number of the Pleiades, the number of the Elder Planets of Astrology, the Seven Sacred Vowels and the Seven Major Chakras within the subtle bodies. This is also the number of synthesis, having moved from the harmonious balance of the number six to a point of gathering all of those experiences into a place of multiple options and outcomes for further expression and exploration. In astrology, the seventh house if often associated with Higher learning.

Location on the Tree

The Polarized Field

Fig. 14

The importance of the interaction between Netzach and Hod is found in the placement of these spheres as being the first linear points on ascending the Tree. Being the polarized opposite of Hod, Netzach is able to provide the necessary refinement of pure intellect. Each interacts directly upon the other; the path between serving as the channel of filter as the flow of energies are moved back and forth. Each sphere carries within itself a replication of the entire Tree, and in this configuration, each of the spheres at polar extremes of pure essence draw some of the other's energies into their core of being.

Base of Pillar of Mercy

Netzach sits at the base of the Pillar of Mercy (Force). It receives the downpour from Chesed (Mercy through knowledge of all the spiritual virtues) and Chokmah (The Celestial Father of Wisdom). It is the ending place of Divine compassion that has been finely honed and created through emanation from the Higher Spheres. Netzach holds within itself the action of response to creativity.

Wisdom-Universal Law

The downpour from those spheres above, when finally arriving within the abode of Netzach have gathered and drawn down into Netzach the appropriate and necessary reactions to knowledge of the Universal Laws. Additionally, they have achieved the state of supreme Wisdom in exercising them (Chokmah) and Mercy (Chesed) that has been drawn from knowledge of the divine virtues that test the limits and boundaries of right action.

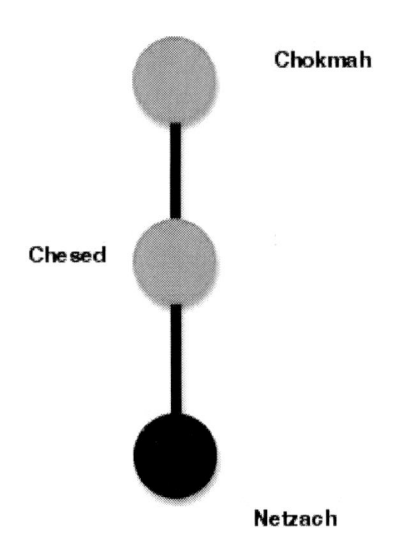

The Pillar of Mercy

Fig. 15

Chokmah	Vision of God	Mercy- Memory
Chesed	Vision of Love	Emotion- Love
Netzach	Vision of Beauty	Triumph

Capacity of the Heart

Netzach also has multiple paths of connection. It, like its opposite sphere Hod is connected via Paths to Tiphareth (the central sphere of the Tree); to the left to Hod (the base sphere of the Pillar of Severity) and to one reaching upwards out of the moon sphere of Yesod. These paths offer many routes of emanation from Netzach's core to be opened and awakened. In its upward movement towards

Chesed, the order and elegance found within Netzach's domain is drawn into Chesed as a higher amplification of the principle of Divine Love. In its descent towards Malkuth, Netzach brings in the energies of compassion and the opportunity for higher expression of physical love.

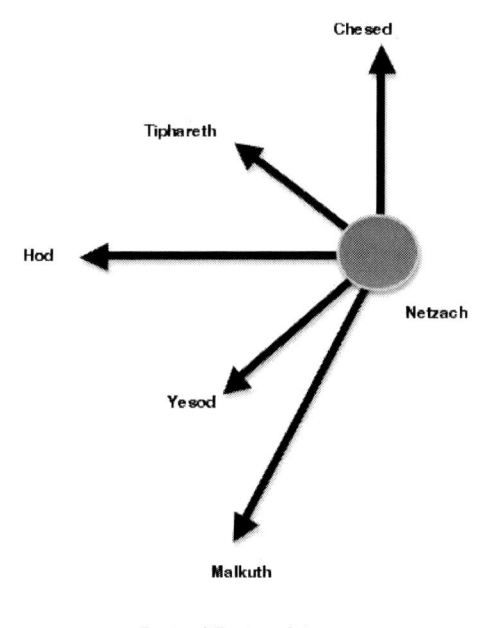

Rays of Expression

Fig. 16

The Spiritual Experience
Vision of Beauty Triumphant

In the sphere of Netzach the vision of beauty is that of nature and all of its components, human, animal, mineral and plant life. There is also a sense of appreciation of all the finer things and the highest ideals. This is present in both the physical concepts of the sphere as well as the spiritual etherical levels. This is the place of triumph over the baser self. Of organized effort to bring refinement and the orphic delights of the arts to fill the container or structure that is being created before it is released into the place of the intellect that can further define and order it.

The Illusion of the Sphere
Lust, Promiscuity

The Illusion of Netzach is that of lust and promiscuity. The highly idealized and divinely infused love contained within the sphere of Netzach can readily be used as a means of only gratifying oneself under the guise of spiritual practice. Many an unscrupulous spiritual leader has seduced the unwitting practitioner into sexual servitude by promising a way to higher enlightenment through the energies of the sex act.

In reality, the sacred sexual practice of Tantric Yoga would fall within the sphere of Netzach. In contrast to the vice of the sphere, in this practice of Tantra, sexual union and the highly refined and potent energies it produces are solely used for the purpose of spiritual development and benefit with the practitioners receiving very specific trainings in technique and undergoing various levels of initiation.

The Briatic Color
Emerald Green

The Magickal Image
A Beautiful Naked Young Woman

The image of a beautiful naked young woman as magickal symbol for Netzach carries with it both appeal to the visual senses and the stimulation of desire for that which is pleasing to the eye and ripe with potential for possessing as one's own. It is the feeding of this desire that causes the will to move beyond stasis and inertia. It is the desire for that which is uplifting that has given the world some of the most beautiful art work. Art work which has been enjoyed for centuries and is lasting. And, it is the desire for permanence which Netzach infuses Hod's brilliant flashes of inspired thought with that gives way to lasting manifestations.

Expression Through The Four Worlds

Continuing the insight referenced in Hod and adding the energetic color of Netzach take another look at the color attributions of the spheres through the four worlds. As stated previously, there is an interesting pattern and cross relationship that carries through with the thought that the Tree occurs simultaneously in multiple replications of itself within each of the spheres.

In the Assiac world Yellow and Gold run through each of the spheres thus far. And at the level of Atziluth, the spheres of Malkuth and Netzach share a base of yellow (Amber is yellow and brown) and Yesod and Hod each have a deep red undertone; Indigo being red and blue and Violet Purple being red, blue and a touch of yellow in base. See how many cross connections you can make. *(For the complete list, see pgs. 26-27)*

	Malkuth	Yesod	Hod	Netzach
Atziluth	Yellow	Indigo	Violet Purple	Amber
Yetzirah	Russet, Black Citrine and Olive	Violet	Russet Red	Emerald Green
Briah	Black, Russet Citrine and Olive flecked Gold	Very Dark Purple	Orange	Bright Yellowish Green
Assiah	Black, with Rays of Olive and Yellow	Citrine flecked with Azure	Yellowish Brown flecked with Gold	Olive flecked with Gold

Atziluth - The Creative Urge
The Supreme Lord of Life
Deity of Beauty and Love
Egyptian- Hathor- Lady of Music, the Arts and Love
Greek - Aphrodite - Goddess of Love

In the sphere of Hod, Atziluth was exemplified in the archetypical energy of those Deities who provide the essence of thought and idea in its most pure and abstract sense. To balance and refine this pure thought, Netzach within the world of Atziluth offers the place of the Orphic Path. Intellect without the balance and containment of emotion seeds the potential for dogma and irreverence and disregard for the human aspects and needs. This aspect of creative urge fosters the yearning and desire for union of the mind and the heart at a mid point where each is fed and nurtured by the other and the downpour of manifest progeny can begin.

As exemplified by the Goddess Aphrodite, love is the basis of all creation. It is in love that the Divine splits in the polarized outpour of male and female, mind and heart. It is in love that we find the elements needed to soar above our own limited personality and it is in love that if mind or rationale and heart or feeling are co-joined and working collaboratively that we bring the highest form of this combined effort into being.

Briah - Creation of a Concept - Archangel
Archangel Haniel
"The Glory of God"

The Archangel Haniel is associated with lunar energies and our natural instincts, passions and creative urge. Haniel's work is to bring us to the place of recognizing our own inner beauty and divinity. This is the lesson of the heart and the balance of duality through polarization. This occurs within the work of synthesis between Hod and Netzach, the mind and heart. As the greater light and beauty is revealed then we see more clearly the place we hold as manifest reflections of the Gods and Goddesses. Healing is also one of the attributes of Haniel. Healing at the level of transforming what was cut away by the sword of Michael in the sphere of Hod. And, the ultimate healing that occurs from self-acceptance.

Yetzirah - Forming the Image of the Concept
Angels - Elohim - God

Netzach is the life force that gives essence to what would otherwise be only lifeless form and reason. With Netzach's energy of the Elohim, the Gods who sired the progeny of the Beni Elohim (sons of the Gods), working in conjunction with the natural emanation into the pure intellect of Hod, thought now has a "reason" to come to life. All of these "children", however, are the result of the polarizing effects of the union of male and female energy constructs. These are Divine thoughtforms, born of polarized Divine consciousness that have come down to a place of being more readily available to the expanded human consciousness.

This life force is the result of the multiple paths or facets of expression in Netzach of the One source of Divinity. This Singular Source has within this sphere moved to an expression through the many and varied Gods. At this level the One has become many. With this thought comes the opportunity for multiple levels of connection to the sphere of Netzach. Each facet is unique and highly specialized in its energy, and because of this the energies of emotion and feeling must be utilized as the selective and driving urge towards union.

Assiah - The World of Expression - Planetary
Venus (Nogah)

The planet Venus was called *Phosphorus* by the Greeks which translates to "Lightbearer" and *Nogah* in Hebrew which means "The Shiner". Venus shines most brightly in the sky in the morning. In the Assiatic World, Netzach is the light that illuminates and refines the mind stream of Hod. Its action is one of enlivening and empowering Hod to reach its fullest potential of expression. Just as Venus is at its brightest at the beginning of the day, Netzach is the first impulse and place of outpour towards the illumined mind. It is both the light that shines at the onset of ascending the Tree, having drawn the energies of pure thought from Hod upwards in distribution towards un-manifest form. And is the light received just before the carefully constructed mind of ideas begins its descent downward towards the filtering energies of Yesod.

The Living Tree: Personal Study

Opening to the Feeling SELF

This set of exercises is intended to make you more aware of the impact of our emotions on the thoughts we hold on to and how they can be used as effective tools towards self-knowledge, growth and dialogue with all parts of our spiritual and human natures.

Journaling: Describe your moment of "Victory"

Select a time in your life when you felt you had great insight and clarity into a situation. The word "victory" in this sense relates to moving through the illusion of what you think is true and seeing and sensing a deeper level of meaning and understanding from this newly opened perspective of emotion. As you write about this experience, allow any additional insights that you may have to flow smoothly and without analysis.

Then, after finishing, go back and take a look at what you have written. How do you "feel" about what you have written? How much more clarity or definition can you add to this writing. What new insights arise as you read through what you have written. Do this for several more iterations. Finally, go back to the beginning writing and make note of the differences, additions, and deletions you may have made after spending some time looking more deeply at the underlying emotions that fueled this scenario.

Chapter Five

TIPHARETH

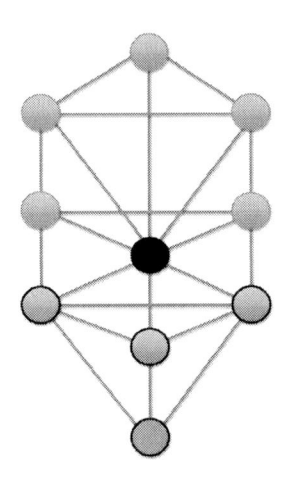

BEAUTY

You are the heat of the
Blazing sun and the cool embers
Of the blue flame that lay
Concealed within.

Potency of magnetic cohesion
And polarity of electrical
Discharge are held within
Your vessel of mysteries.

I surrender to your down pour
I tremble as your force expands
I am blinded by the gnosis
Within your core.

I willingly give my all to
Be filled with the heat of
Your luminosity and
Your strength supports each
Cell of my fragile being.

I remember the mysteries of sacrifice
And my spirit moves within the
Molten core of the many streams
Your fiery essence reveals.

All hail to the redemption of
Man's feeble will that makes clear the
Way as I open to the flaming star of golden
Light and lay claim to the kingship
That becomes my mantle of grace.

The Lesson of the Sphere

Keywords

Harmony
Bliss/Chaos
Conductor/Receptor
Pulse

The Energy of the Sphere

Communion with The Higher and Lower Selves

"As above, So Below"

The sphere of Tiphareth is the central core of the Self. It both emanates its sustaining and strengthening energy and also serves to contract, assimilate and quicken. This energy is magnetic in nature and as it absorbs and draws towards itself, it simultaneously releases, distributes and emits the newly transformed energy. This action is very similar to the process of the heart within the physiology of our being. The heart serves to cleanse and purify the blood for recycling and release to those vital areas that are reached via the elaborate network of vein and artery. This action puts the body in a state of attunement, so that the vital nutrients may be received and the body will remain viable, strong and healthy in function. Tiphareth acts as the place of attunement and synthesis of return and release whereby the energies of the other spheres have a place of common meeting ground to blend and distribute in accord with the specific needs of balance and equilibrium.

Tiphareth is not only the place of deeper connection but it takes that connection further in the call to be "fully present". Fully present in the sense of the bright light of the sun shining on you, moving you into the spotlight and making you accountable not only for showing up to do the work, but to do so in an illuminated and fully enlivened way.

Ascending the Tree, we transcend the limitations of human form and evolve towards a state of pure being of Light. On descent, the Light that emanates from Kether reaches down into Tiphareth and is harmonized by drawing on the qualities of the surrounding spheres. It continues its movement downwards into the density of concrete form, carrying with it the seeds of the previous spheres' energies.

The Consciousness of Consciousness

The energy of Tiphareth is one of Consciousness becoming aware of its own state of Consciousness. At a human level, it is through the inflow and outflow process that we form conclusions, make declarations and define our realities and boundaries of extension. At the level of Tiphareth it is the realization of the Divine nature of our consciousness, its potential and inherent connection to the highly refined powers and principles that emanate from the spheres above as well as the roots of manifestation and form that lay below. This becomes the cornerstone of Devotion. As is the nature of everything within Tiphareth's domain there is the duality of the more dense realization of that devotion and the higher aspiration and meaning of that word in connection with The Great Work. That Great Work becomes the intimate work of one's self, thus affecting your personal and spiritual evolvement and cultivating the end result of expression of refined Devotion demonstrated by effectively doing your Great Work of Spirit within the world.

The Mediating Intelligence

The Synthesis of the Energy of Existence

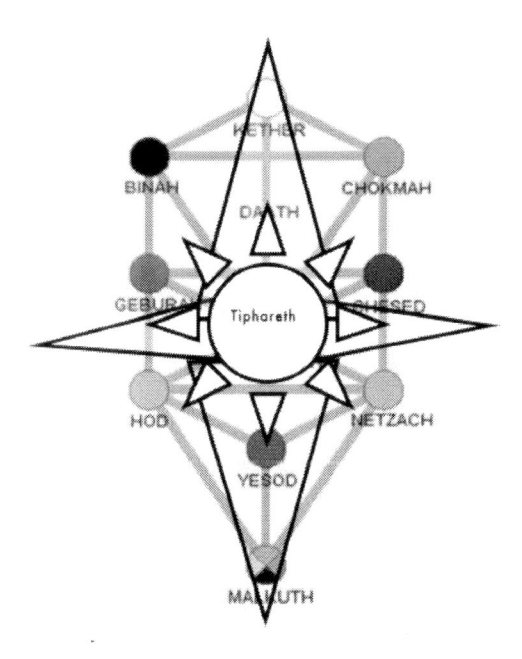

Fig. 17

Soul and Body, Self and Ego, Higher Consciousness and Personality come together magnetically, electrically and willfully in a meeting of Higher Consciousness and Refined Personality before ascending upwards towards the Supernal spheres or drawing that synthesis downwards towards the human experience of Malkuth. When we "mediate" we act from a place of bridging and standing between; not giving more emphasis or credence to one thing over another. A decision in favor of one side may be made, but only after carefully weighing the differences and similarities of the opposing sides. This is the action of Tiphareth. Holding many paths of influence in steady balance and sorting and acting upon the varied influences as they present. This vantage point of being centrally located also gives a greater perspective to each of its connecting paths and spheres. One that is illuminated by the combined Light and Truth of each acting as a hub around which the Universe of ideas, thoughtforms and energies revolve.

The Solar Principle of Energetic Awakening

Kundalini and Tiphareth

If we consider Tiphareth from the perspective of its solar energy and enlivening qualities it is not too far a stretch to map that similar energy onto the process of personal energetic alchemy. The fundamental principles of the awakening of Kundalini energy are that of the combining of the solar (Pingala/Surya) principles and the lunar (Ida/Chandra) as they intersect specific chakras in an upward ascent up the Sushumna (the central column that runs just behind the spinal column vertically from the perineum up through the crown of the head). These pathways are referred to as the Nadis. The Nadis (the Sanskrit word for "tube, pipe") are the channels through which, in traditional Indian medicine and spiritual science, the energies of the subtle body are said to flow. They connect at the specific points or vortices of energy called chakras.

We can overlay this energy onto the Middle Pillar of the Qabalistc Tree, which is the direct route of access to the brilliance of Kether.

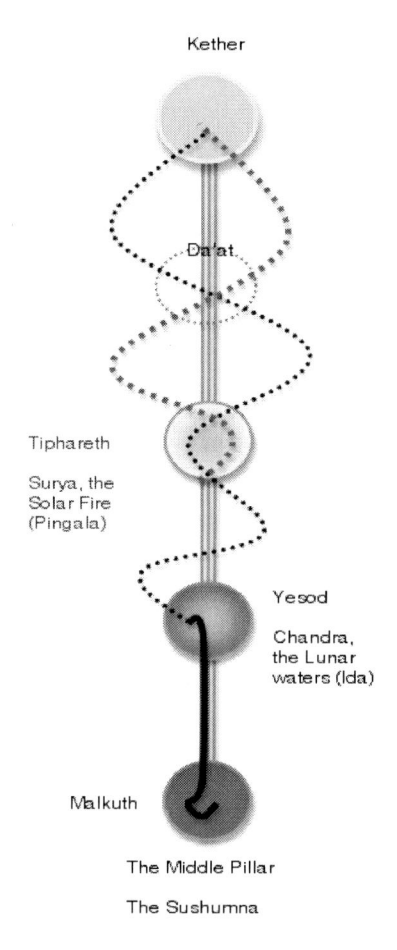

Fig. 18

The Ida/Chandra (moon) or lunar energy

And

The Pingala/Surya (solar principle)solar energy

Rise up the Sushumna (central column) to a higher state of union with the Divine

The work of spiritual aspiration is to follow the Middle Way, moving through the sphere of Yesod, up and through Tiphareth, crossing the abyss of Da'at and reaching the finality of Kether. In using these same qabalistic principles we could liken this journey to that of a Kundalini awakening. In this format the Lunar or Chandra energy emanates from Yesod. As it moves upwards and comes to the gates of Tiphareth, this energy entwines and is quickened by the breath (remember the attribute of Air associated with Tiphareth and Yesod) of life fires from Tiphareth, the solar principle. In this domain, the lunar and the solar principles merge, blend and synthesize, before moving upwards on their continued paths. They would most likely cross again at Da'at (this is the sphere of the shadow self and the final release of those parts of self that are not in union with the Higher State of Being). Once again, each moves upward until they reach their final place of union and illumination within the sphere of Kether, the place of the All.

Now, this is all speculation, but when we learn to think of the attributes and energies of the Tree is conjunction with that knowledge which we can grasp and bring into a physical experience we have a greater understanding of the way in which the Tree of Life is mapped onto and scaled into everything, at all levels of being.

The Element of the Sphere
Air

Tiphareth is assigned the element of Air. One might question this as much of the attributions of Tiphareth center around the Sun and solar energies contained within. But, if we think in an esoteric sense, the energy of air is the same as that catalytic force that breathed the world into creation through speaking the word. It is through breath that the words of power are uttered and manifestation pours forth. So, if we hold this context in mind, Tiphareth is the place of manifestation of the new life breathed into each of the energies that move through and out of it.

Numerical Value

Tiphareth is the **Sixth** Sphere. Within the energy of the number **6** lies the harmonious relationship between the essential trinity and the spiritually amplified trinity of Higher expression. As we work within a state of balance and sincerity of action designed towards the higher good for all we move towards a place of spiritual enlightenment. This is the call to bring into harmony and collaborative interaction the synthesized product of compassion and forgiveness. This is the sacrifice of one's pride and ego that is necessary to put the momentum of devotion to the Great Work in process.

Location on the Tree

Sits Centrally On the Middle Pillar of Equilibrium

Kether

Yesod

Malkuth

The Middle Pillar
Pillar of Equilibrium

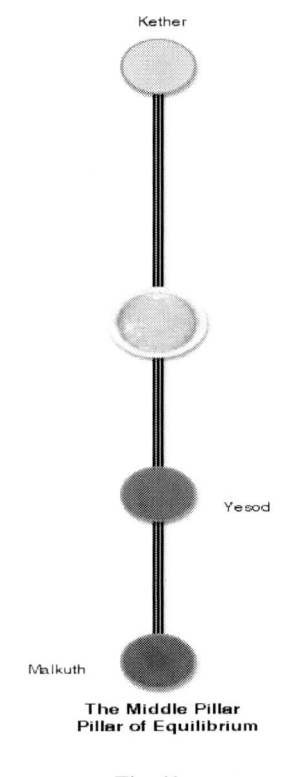

Fig. 19

Strategically placed at the center of the Middle Pillar of Equilibrium, Tiphareth has a panoramic view in all directions. It also has the distinction of being the place of that which divides the lower half and upper half of the Tree. That which is manifest and denser in matter and form must first pass through the heat of Tiphareth before it can be exhaled towards the heavens and the more refined natures of the upper spheres.

Intersected by 8 Paths

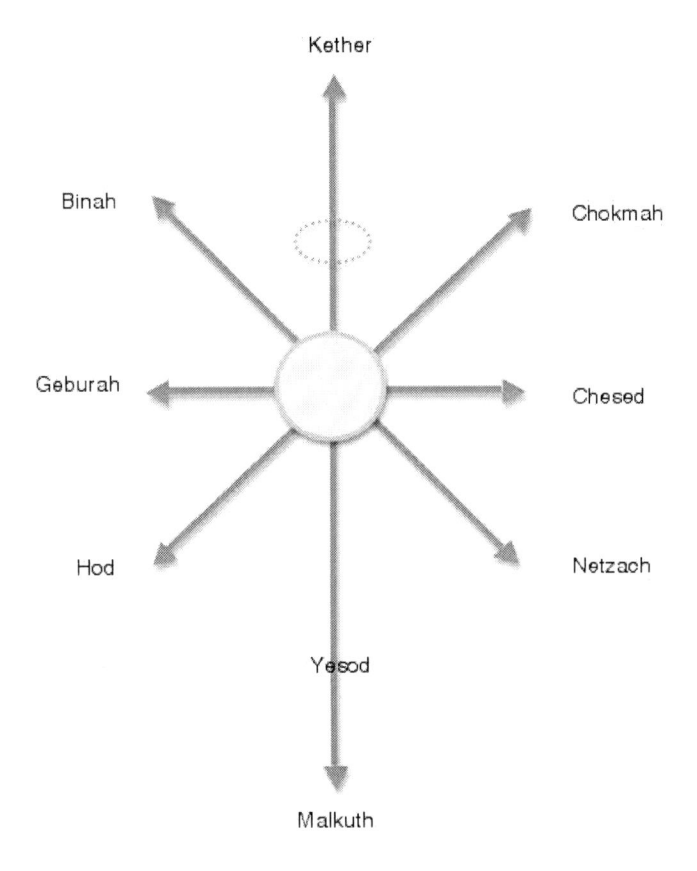

Fig. 20

At the level of Tiphareth the PATHS become the Living means of conducting energy to and from the Central Source devoid of their attributes and codifications. Each of the spheres, as they proceed into the heart of Tiphareth becomes less identifiable of its own nature as it blends with and establishes a place of collaborative energetic flow, one to the other. None being more important than the other, and all being of great necessity for the overall output.

The Outpour of the 8 Pathways

The emanation of energy flows from:

Yesod: The creative image board from which conclusion can be formulated.
Hod: Decoding of Symbols, Metaphor and the Illusions of Yesod and communication.
Netzach: Intelligence of the Heart. The combining of pure thought and compassionate grace.
Geburah: The necessary release and rebirth.
Chesed: The broader perspective and keen discernment.
Binah: The womb that gives form to what is formless.
Chokmah: The first impulse and creation towards duality.
Kether: The infinite Source that both begins and ends the process.

The Spiritual Experience
The Vision Of Harmony and Of Sacrifice

In the previous chapter, it was stated that the spiritual experience of Netzach was the Vision of Beauty Triumphant. This "beauty" was that of all of nature and its components. When we arrive at the level of Tiphareth, this vision becomes one of the harmony underlying that which has been organized into something of beauty. The sum of all its parts has come together in just the right manner to produce that which is harmonious, has integrity and is whole. This is the first glimpse of our Higher Self, the pure intuitive self that has established a finely tuned working collaboration between the personal and manifest needs of the individual and the greater desires of spirit. Leaving behind those manifest and physical attributes that are not in alignment with our higher state of being that we so fiercely cling to are often regarded as sacrifices. This is the illusion, for the place of sacrifice is not held within the material world, but much deeper within the Soul where desire is driven by the individual personality and is only achieved in letting go of that personality to become at once singular and part of the greater whole. That is the expression of humanity in its Divine place of Kingship.

The Illusion of the Sphere
Identification

We, as humans like to label ourselves and often seek approval, attention or simply community through the identification we make with those groups, energies, personality traits, etc. Identifying with specific things is not in itself a negative attribute, but when we very strongly confine and bind our being within that identity to the exclusion of acceptance or consideration of another way this creates a lack of movement or stasis within our being.

The illusion of Tiphareth is one of cutting off the flow of outside input. Of so strongly seeing itself as being of only one nature and fabric in its energetic expression that the magnetism ceases and the smooth continuum of informed flow stops and is backed up into itself. At this juncture everything implodes from the sheer force of misdirected energy. Take pride in what you wish to claim as your own, but allow the flow of what is not to pass through as well. Often within that flow of what we think is not ours to identify with are found the smallest pieces of gold that open the doors to greater collaboration and draw like the magnet of Tiphareth your inner gold back to the Source.

The Briatic Color
Golden Yellow

The Magickal Image
A Child, A Majestic King and a Sacrificed God

The images that are attributed to the sphere of Tiphareth may seem to have no connection at all on first glance. A child, a King and a sacrificed God seem as incongruous to be placed in a triad of empowerment as to combine the forces of a dancer, an artist and an engineer. But, as with many endeavors it is the collaborative efforts of each bringing their own particular piece to the puzzle that creates the masterpiece that would have lain uncreated had they not looked deeper for the common as well as the differences inherent within each.

The child in this case is our point of birth. The place of origin where all potentiality is imbued within a life and light filled being, before the impact and influence of the world is set upon him/her. The child knows nothing other than unconditional Love and sees the world in its true form of light and magick. The inner beauty and light of everything is revealed and there is untapped strength, that if fostered and nurtured (Binah, the Great Mother), then acknowledged and honed from a diverse perspective (Chokmah) will serve the child as he matures.

The Majesty of the King is the natural process for this child. Having garnered and gathered from years of experience and selectively and carefully weeded those things that served no productive ends (Geburah), authority and the process of wielding this power is held within his command. If the lessons have been learned well, compassion (Netzach) will grace those decisive moments.

And, there will come a point of testing, a Dark Night of the Soul (Da'at) when the King's true worth and aspiration is put to the fires. Intellect (Hod) and drawing upon the lessons of the storehouse of knowledge (Yesod) will be critical to this process. This is the place of turning point and choice of dedication to the Greater Work that serves all and the ALL, or choosing the path upon which he will remain as a King only.

If the choice is made to step into the place of greater Kingship, the King of Majesty and right becomes the Sacrificed One. He becomes in human eyes a God for he has set aside personality and ego and has embraced the individualized self that has achieved union with the Divine. This choice has been offered at great sacrifice, but has been made willingly and shows us that we must lay aside our separate (individual) lives to achieve the ultimate union with the Divine Source and the All. This Sacrificed God is the attainment and awareness of our Higher Self in balance with our place among humanity.

So, you see, the work of great acclaim was achieved when the artist provided the visual backdrop, which inspired the dancer to choreograph a performance piece which required the skill and knowledge of the engineer to design the set that would allow the dancer to safely and gracefully fly, seemingly in mid-air, as she moved across the blazing sun of Tiphareth painted by the artist.

Expression Through The Four Worlds

Atziluth - The Creative Urge

The Supreme Lord of Life
The Solar and Deities of Sacrifice
Egyptian: RA-Osiris
Greek - Apollo

In the sphere of Tiphareth, Atziluth is exemplified in the archetypical energy of those Deities who provide the light of sustaining form and those who represent the sacrifice inherent in rising above the lower aspects of form. When we think of RA and Apollo, the Sun and its glory of radiance and light come to mind. These Gods also had the triune phase of that solar cycle as part of their energetic purpose. It is Khepra-RA we greet at the dawn of day, the youth who is just beginning to bring the glory of his light to earth. Amun-RA holds reign over the noonday sun as full peak and majestic glory of the King. But, in the evening as darkness returns once again it is Atum-RA in the form of the sacrificial Lord, who must diminish to the underworld (a proverbial death) for renewed life and quickening during the night's time of balance and synthesis before he may return once again as the illumined light of day. If this death did not occur; if this sacrifice was not made the balance of night and day would be overturned and its loss mourned.

Osiris, is the supreme sacrificial God and through his re-membering by Isis (Queen of Magick and the Night in one of her forms) becomes the Light of the midnight Sun that sits within the darkness of the underworld. It is by his grace that RA may arise again each morning. This is the ultimate work of Tiphareth in Atziluth; to ensure the balance.

Briah - Creation of a Concept- Archangel
Archangel Raphael and Michael
"Glory of God"

The Archangels Raphael and Michael are associated with the creative aspect of Tiphareth. Their task is to bring into view the aspects of those who are considered the heroes, the saviors and the saints. Michael brings Fire to the creative process and Raphael provides the air that feeds the flame of Michael's creative fires. Being the master of the Light, Raphael also provides the state of illumination necessary after the wanton destruction of those principles and ideals that are not in alignment with the concept of the "perfected" man. This "perfected" man is one who is no longer bound by physical matter and having the wings of grace bestowed by the archangels to the worthy has the potential to ascend upwards towards union with the Divine Source of all being. Michael provides the spark of Life necessary to quicken. Together they forge the fires of desire to achieve a state of illumined form. Air fans the Flame and the Flame ever spires towards the Heavens.

Yetzirah - Forming the Image of the Concept

Angels - Malachim

" The Angelic Kings"

The Malakim(chim) are considered the angels of balance and centralization. As they go about their work they bring authority and kingship to the equilibrium that is established. This state of balance is not necessarily of each part weighing the same to arrive at a state of equal exertion. This is the balance that flows when there is continued flow, one from and to the other, allowing movement and interaction to be equalizer. All is in a constant state of change around them, so their job is to provide the points of balance for the action of change itself so that a minimum of disharmony occurs. They may be considered the "checks and balances" that ensure there will not be overload, thus causing chaos in any one area of action. They are also responsible for the form and structure of whatever the place of synthesizing and organizing may be and how that form and shape relates to those other things impacted by and surrounding the original concept.

Assiah - The World of Expression - Planetary

The Sun

The Sun, just as the Moon of Yesod, holds dual meaning within the sphere of Tiphareth. Its energy is both that of the physical sun and all of the correlates that describe that body of energy as well as the esoteric meaning of the Greater Sun and its mysteries that lay behind what we see physically.

Within the physical domain of the Sun, its energies are that of being a source and sustainer of life as we know it on this planet. Light and heat are necessary and vital components to existence of all living things. It is central to the world of our particular Universe and scope. However, if we were to move too close to that same sustaining Light and heat we would perish in flame. Matter returning to the state of formless, pure energy.

Esoterically, the Sun is seen as the Light of Reason. The grand illuminator that provides the spark or nuclei of energy necessary to cause creation. The Sun behind the Sun, is the place of the Greater Mysteries. The birthing place and point of origin of all spiritual action. Just as in the physical sense, with the light of day everything is seen in a clearer state; so too within the greater light of the spiritual sun clarity of purpose, intent and the Source of all Life is revealed.

In spiritual practice, the Sun of Tiphareth is the call to finding and balancing the light that emanates from within, and from which all other experiences of growth and purpose are renewed. Once this place is activated and empowered, the Greater Light is drawn towards you as the magnetized energy of the Sun and the mystery of your inner Light is revealed for all to see.

The Living Tree: Personal Study

Opening to Beauty

This set of exercises is intended to make you more aware of the places in our lives that have called for an action of sacrifice and the effects it had on the resulting final outcome.

Journaling: Facing Your Place of Sacrifice

- Think back to a time in your life when you felt you had sacrificed something you had strongly held on to. Bring this image clearly into the mind's eye and allow the scenario to play out in front of you on your inner screen.

- When the image is clear and strong, begin to write about this experience. Write down all that you remember in as much detail as possible. As you write about this experience, allow to flow any additional insights that you may have.

- Then, after finishing, go back and take a look at what you have written. Add to this the thoughts and perceptions you have now regarding the situation. What would you have done differently? Would you have made the same choices or would you have held more tightly to what was given up?

- As you think on these questions, allow the writing to simply flow. Do not concern yourself with grammar or spelling or even putting into coherent sentences. Just allow the words to flow and build in whatever manner they choose.

- When you have finished. Close your journal and allow the thoughts to sit over night. Do not give any more conscious thought to what you wrote. At your next available time, reread what you wrote. Find the places of beauty within what transpired within the scenario of sacrifice you described. Make note of whatever, if any, changes you would have made. Trust in the inner strength and courage that you showed at that time and gather the wisdom you recently crafted into the scenario towards this inner strength you have cultivated now. These are the keys to transformation and new approach towards those things we wish to "willingly" give way to so that something of beauty may be born from it.

Chapter Six

GEBURAH

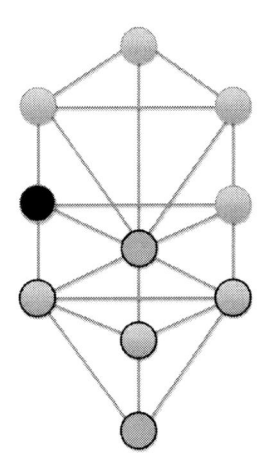

MIGHT

I sit shivering in the dark
Eyes closed and all of my being
Filled with fear that I will
Lose my most valued possession.

Flame and heat surround
Yet the air is dense with
Energy that moves like
Cold steel wielded by a
Forceful hand.

What I cling to so fiercely
I have long ago outgrown
But the comfort and safety

Provided are like soothing
Ointment on wounds that
Have yet to be opened.

I want to be free of these chains
I want to be whole
What I carry are bits and pieces
Of my own folly and the thought of
Excision sends me into retreat.

As reason gives way to desire
And understanding stands at the
Threshold with outstretched hand
I rise from this place of cowering
I open my eyes to see what lay
Ahead and a cold dark hand
Grasps my own as I look into
The eyes of myself.

The only demons I have to fear is what
Lay within the spectre of my shadow
With the single act of embrace
All that is to be discarded
Falls from me
I am Free.

I am strong and what I had
Feared losing the most
Has only been transformed
And forged anew
The dark gives way to light and
I step forward to greet the
Final outcome.

The Lesson of the Sphere

Keywords

Resistance
Justice
Strength
Choice/Free Will/Discernment
Justice

The Energy of the Sphere

It is with the precision of a surgeon's scalpel or the more radical aggression of the soldier wielding the sword that the imbalance of disease or disharmony of unchecked (unrestrained) power is excised, reshaped and transmuted by the catalytic energy of Geburah.

The sphere of Geburah is probably the most feared sphere on the Tree. It is also largely the most misunderstood or misinterpreted as its energy is fierce in nature, accepting nothing less than change and exerts a force that is transformative. If you look at the energy of Geburah and see its balance on the pillar of Mercy, the sphere of Chesed, it is easier to see exactly why things must be exactly as they are in the realm of Geburah. This dynamic flow of energetic alchemy is precisely what is needed for spiritual growth.

On ascending the Tree, having moved from the harmony and balance of Tiphareth and arriving in Geburah we are now faced with choice and free will. Geburah is the place of creating and exercising discernment. Knowing when to push the limits and how to create the necessary resistance to the surge of creativity that provides boundaries to create form from what has potential to become chaos. It is through this process of movement, force, challenge, obstacle and friction that we have the greatest potential for growth and greater free will of a higher frequency that is more Spiritual in nature and further away from the mundane plane and limitations of Malkuth.

The energy of Geburah gives us courage to see with more clarity. With that courage there is a necessary caution that arises as we continue towards building a space of strength from which to exert the force and action that is needed. This is a place of wise caution that takes the form of reverence for that which is greater than ourselves and using only enough force necessary to purge that which we should versus the proverbial "throwing the baby out with the bathwater"

When we begin to trust our abilities to make wise choices about what must be released and what lends itself to transformation we begin the first steps towards drawing upon the guidance of the Higher Self. The Self that is devoid of ego and guided by the merciful (Chesed) in seeing the bigger picture and thus, allowing that which must fall to the wayside to do so with the strength of knowing it is for the greater good.

The Rooted Consciousness

The energy of Geburah is one of Consciousness that is both unified and productive. One of its direct points of emanation is from Binah (Understanding). Binah holds within its energy that of true understanding and comprehension having come from the Source of Kether. In this way, Geburah serves as anchor for this stream of understanding and provides the filtering point from which the denser manifestation of that understanding can emanate into the lower spheres of experience. It is thus rooted in the energy of the Higher spheres and subject to their laws and Will.

The Radical Intelligence

The sphere of Geburah is designated as the Radical Intelligence. **By definition the word radical means:**

1. Of or from the roots; going to the foundation or source of something [as in a radical principle].

2. Extreme; thorough [as in a radical change].

3. Favoring fundamental or extreme change, especially in socio-economic structure.

4. (noun) **A basic or root part of something.**

If we think of these definitions in terms of intelligence or the act of "knowing" it is evident that in order to successfully change or modify something there should be a basic understanding (Binah) of the workings, principles and energies of that thing. Once these "knowings" have been established the excision can be made and healing and new growth are just ahead. This is also the point where response to the boundaries that have been created by this informed intelligence can be distributed either in the manner of what appears to be the extreme of what is currently held in place or with justified reservation.

The Element of the Sphere

Fire

Geburah is assigned the element of Fire, which unlike the other elements cannot exist in physical form without consuming and destroying something else, thus causing transformation of that thing. It is out of that destruction that the potential for the most growth often occurs. Like the legendary Phoenix rising from the flames of ash, the work of Geburah is to heat things up, and at this level, it carries the seeds of change that are the stuff of initiatory transformation, action and development of the Higher Will.

Numerical Value

Geburah is the **Fifth** Sphere. Within the energy of the number **5** is the regenerative process and the potential for directing that energy towards a specific and defined goal of new creation. When we arrive at the number five, we have opened up the stable base of four; visualize a square. Something has disrupted the order of that four and made way for a new form to appear. We see also the number five as represented by the Pentagram. Five points, each reflective of a quality of an element (fire, water, air and earth) and at the pinnacle or point, the element of Spirit. Spirit being the essence and sum total containing all of the basic elements within it and transformed to a point of focus and direction, reaching ever upwards towards the higher experiences of Spirit as revealed through Kether.

Location on the Tree

The Middle Sphere On the Middle Pillar of Severity

Binah
I Understand

Geburah
I Render

Hod
I Reason

The Mid-Point
of
The Pillar of Severity

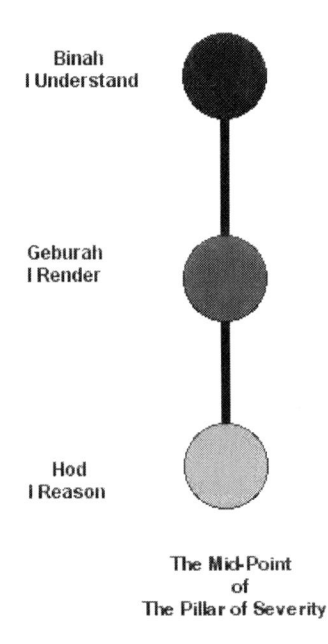

Fig. 21

Strategically placed at the center of the Middle Pillar of Severity Geburah receives the downpour from Binah and the upward striving of Hod's energy. If we equate Binah with understanding and Hod with reason, we can think of Geburah as being the central activator that takes in both streams of emanation, transforms them through its creative and disruptive action and renders them useable. This is the "tough mother" who takes into consideration the logic of her child's folly and has empathy from having traveled the same road herself and finally from a place of ultimate love does what is necessary in whatever way is necessary to make this lesson a remembered one. And, depending upon the severity of the action the extremes that may be taken on her part will be in the form of both judge and juror.

Choice and Free Will

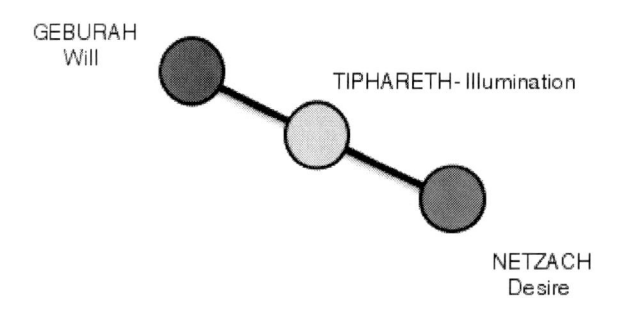

Fig. 22

So, if we look at the scenario outlined above, you may wonder where choice and free will come into play. If we consider Geburah and the energy it receives on the diagonal path through Tiphareth and emanating from Netzach, we see the end release of these prior potent energies. Netzach is the place of desire in its stages of initializing the energy needed for action upon what we desire. I equate it to some degree with the raw need and desire for a particular thing. Exerting your will to claim that something and then taking the necessary steps leading up to the resolved and successful acquisition of that desire.

If, however, we move that initial will up into Tiphareth we gain more insight and illumination or light on what is the true nature of the object of our desire, and because information is being gathered from a variety of sources (remember Tiphareth stands as the central receiver of all of the spheres' energies) we now have many more informed choices about how to proceed.

As this desire moves forward into the realms of Geburah, the need to organize and reform and toss aside those options that are not viable, mix and match those that are and then pare it down again to become the imminent need. This process is one that calls upon the individual's strength and will to make these choices well informed. And, when the final agreement as to how to proceed is made, action and movement may take hold and choice and free will are the parents of what has been created.

The Energetic Triad

The Energetic Triad
Fire - Water - Air

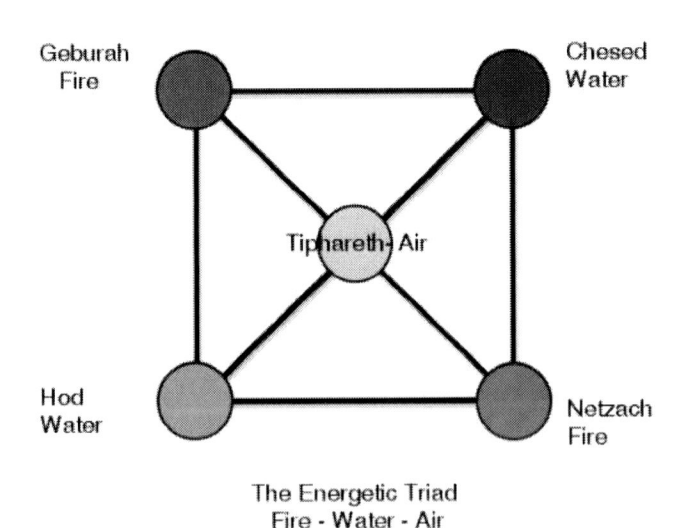

Fig. 23

If we look at any of the three connecting points in Fig. 23 as we move around the perimeter of the square there is a pattern that emerges. The pattern is that of FIRE, WATER and AIR. This triad, or triangle represent the three points of flow and return that form the basis for energetic fire. This thought process is particularly useful if you engage in a regular energetic practice to enliven the spiritual fires within. In each case one of the elements acts as the positive point from which the initializing effects proceed. There is a moment of neutrality or pause where the initial charge is synthesized, transformed and reversed and then outpour or flow towards the point of negative magnetic polarity occurs. The action of positive and negative reacting and acting upon one another creates the electric burst or fire that produces energy.

Through the Medium of Water (neutral point) the potent Directive Energy of Fire (positive) moves to a place of discharge within the organizing, lawful movement of Air (negative) in the space of Aether (energetic vessel of boundary)

For example:

The outpour of desire for beauty and harmonious union (Netzach) moving through the waters of pure mind (Hod) are polarized, acted upon and released by the breath of strength and sacrifice (Tiphareth) to produce informed and unconditional love.

or

The release and creative outpour of Will (Geburah) moving through the waters of pure reason (Hod) are polarized, acted upon and released through the downpour of the sun's light as illumined and informed action.

The Outpour of the 8 Pathways

This bears repeating and now that we know the true nature of Geburah, we can see the importance of the release and transformation that is called for to maintain the flow of balance.

At the level of Tiphareth the PATHS become Living means of conducting energy to and from the Central Source devoid of their attributes and codifications. Each of the spheres as they proceed into the heart of Tiphareth becomes less identifiable as it blends with and establishes a place of collaborative energetic flow, one to the other. None being more important than the other, and all being of great necessity for the overall output.

Take another look at Fig. 20 in Chapter Five (pg. 96).

The Spiritual Experience
The Vision Of Power

The spiritual vision of Geburah is one of power. The immediate response to the word "power" is usually one of awe and feeling as though something great has been won or achieved. It also usually has the connotation of being superior or exerting will over someone or something. These qualities in and of themselves are not necessarily negative of their own accord, but become of a less than higher nature if infused with overinflated and self-indulgent ego. The energy of Geburah in its pure and true sense is one that commands awe and most importantly, respect. Respect for the strength and courage needed to be the ultimate "down-sizer" and awe at the newly formed creation that is its result. This action does bring us to a superior place. Superior in that its energy is that of refined higher spiritual essence; the energy in which we have exerted Will upon to achieve this great vision. It is our lower mind that is driven by the needs of the human ego and personality devoid of spiritual insight. It is with reverence and awe that we hold in thought any of the energies of the Sephiroth and it is with the grace of the Divine and the upholding of our higher state of being that we claim the mantle of Power.

The Illusion of the Sphere
Cruelty, Needless Destruction

When the reformative energy of Geburah takes hold it is not always easy to determine when we have crossed the line from constructive criticism and egging on towards reaching the fullest potential to harsh words of no value and tearing down an individual's self worth. These are some of the pitfalls of the Geburic energy when it is not truly aligned with that which is for the highest good. The power one can exert over another and the Pygmalion-like complex is an alluring one that does much to feed the ego and baser personality of the one in charge. The danger in this is even more potent in that often the person issuing what they believe to be encouragement, albeit in a negative way, may actually believe that it is in the best interest of the one who is receiving this negative outpour. Knowing when and how far to go with critiques and judgment is the hardest lesson of this sphere; but once those boundaries have been established one can truly say that **justified** harshness can truly better the situation.

The Briatic Color
Scarlet

When we see the color red, we feel rejuvenated and stirred to action. Red is the color of blood (when it has been acted upon by air/oxygen) and the life that this fluid running through our bodies brings. Red is also equated with anger and aggression. When we hear the phrase "seeing red" it generally has a negative connotation and avoid whoever is in that state. Interestingly, red is also the color of passion. The imagery of excitement and sexual arousal has provided the cosmetics companies with multi-billion returns in the purchase of ruby red lipstick.

The Magickal Image
"A Mighty Warrior in his Chariot"

The image that is attributed to the sphere of Geburah is that of a mighty warrior in his chariot. In synchronicity, the Tarot card, The Chariot, connects the spheres of Geburah and Binah by way of the 18th Path.

This Path is attributed to water, the zodiacal sign of Cancer and the Moon. The Chariot stands as connection to the Fire of Geburah and the Root of Water that is Binah, The Great Mother. It is within the catalytic energies of these waters that the spark of fire or creative effort pours forth. It is through the dedicated action of exerting control over those parts of ourselves that need reigning in and tempering that the transformed newly forged self may appear.

Expression Through The Four Worlds

Atziluth - The Creative Urge

The Supreme Lord of Life
The Deities of Strength, Power and Avenging Energy

Ares- Kali- Shiva- The Morrigan- Sekhmet

And

Gods and Goddesses of the Forge

Bran- Brighid- Lugh

In the sphere of Geburah, Atziluth is exemplified in the archetypical energy of those Deities who provide the impetus to push us through challenge and release to the place of inevitable change and growth. These are the Deity that cut away, force us to face our darker nature and exert their power and strength when and where we feel the most vulnerable. The irony is that most of these Deity are also directly responsible for the process of healing and rebirth; for it is after all, that from the fields of decay and destruction, new life finds a way. If it were not for the compost of manure and rotting plant and vegetable matter, the beauty of Spring's flowers and succulent life sustaining fruits and vegetables could not be grown. In this aspect these gods and goddesses are not only the destroyers but also those of fertile insemination.

There is another component to this change that is exemplified through the energy of those Deities most closely tied to the fires of the Forge. They take what has been melted down and transformed into a rarified state and from that point of heat craft something that is enduring and may then be used to finish the work of cutting away that was begun.

Briah - Creation of a Concept - Archangel

Archangel Khamael

"The Burner of God"

The Archangel Khameal is often called " The Burner of God" and acts to assist in the process of acquiring through release the skills and tools needed for transformation. He is known as the Angel of Justice and Severity. There is a certain justice that occurs when things are let go of that serve no useful purpose beyond that of serving to fuel the fires of unjust power. The process in which this is done is often severe in nature, but despite the disruption, discord and potential chaos, what then emerges is a new sense of being and a changed perspective of focus that is of better service to the ongoing process. Khameal, with the aid of the Seraphim directs this process.

Yetzirah - Forming the Image of the Concept

Angels - Seraphim

" The Fiery Serpents"

The Seraphim are regarded as being of the highest Order of Angel and are most closely associated with the work of the Archangel under whose guidance and direction they fall. They represent the highest level of judgment and punishment. Symbolically, their sound of issue is represented by a musical chord of condensed flame that is constantly coiling and vibrating in motion.

The Seraphim bring the intensity of heat and direct the focus of Archangel Khameal's transformative energies to burn away what is no longer needed. One of their functions is to remove the useless clutter within our mental and spiritual realms, to make ready for the final release of the human ego as connection with the Divine SELF is pursued. In this way, they become the Serpents of Wisdom that are catalytic in nature and at times ruthless in execution.

Assiah - The World of Expression - Planetary

Mars

The energy of Mars is that of being the corrector of Imbalance, the ultimate equalizer. It is the energy behind a War that strives to bring an end to war, simply because sometimes that is the only way to override a power that is being misused. Anger, aggression and assertiveness are often viewed in our society as being inappropriate and negative behaviors. However, if there were not the fueling of the energetic fires of anger towards the atrocities of child abuse, female mutilation and other social injustices, these injustices and ill-used power plays would go unnoticed and unchanged. The fiery light of Mars shines brightly and brings into the central heat of the flame that which needs transformation.

The Living Tree: Personal Study

Opening to Discernment: Active Engagement

Follow the news for the next three weeks. Identify the Geburic events. How could they be **"Tipharized"**?

Chapter Seven

CHESED

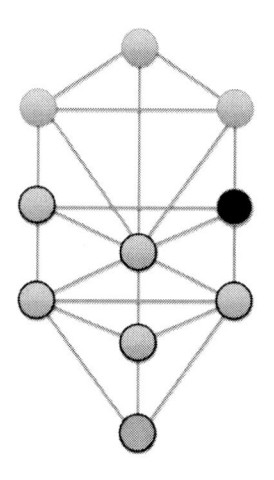

MERCY

Take my hand child
You have come far
And your journey has been
Treacherous.

Come sit beside me
And feel the weight
Of expansion as it moves
Through your being.

Open your eyes
And look down
From the great heights
You have scaled as all
Comes to a precise point.

What once was unfocused
Has sharpened to a gaze of
Crystal clarity.

I offer you sanctuary
But you must walk through the
Heat of transformative
Change before
You come to me.

And if you stand before me
Having declared your
Intent to service the
Threshold shall be opened
And the leap of ultimate faith
Will be your new course.

The Lesson of the Sphere

Keywords

Foundation

Authority and Humility

Divine Power

Moderation

Obedience

The Energy of the Sphere

Chesed is also known as Gedulah or the sphere of love and majesty. As we move through the remaining spheres we can more clearly see that all of the spheres below Kether are variations and permutations of the ONE. This realization can be likened to the importance of correct lighting in a theatrical production. On each of the stage lamps, various colored gel filters are used to refract the brilliance of a singular white stage light in order to create the necessary ambience or mood in support of the action onstage. These slight variations serve to move the consciousness and visual perception of the audience into another reality. For the most part, the beauty of this is that this simple act of refraction of light is done in a transparent way that seamlessly connects with the action, the music and the sets of the production.

Chesed is the last sphere ascending the Tree before crossing the abyss (Da'at) that separates the pure Divine essence of the Supernal (Godhead) Spheres of the Tree. Its energy is that of coalescent and refined summation of the experience afforded the spheres leading up to this point. This sphere is often considered the Hall of the Masters; the point where choice is made to either remain and serve humanity or to ascend beyond the realm of physical expression and be fully reabsorbed into the source of all creation.

Descending the Tree, Chesed is the first sphere of actuality. This is the point where flow and form have merged and become the juncture that is the beginning work towards actualizing the concept or idea of manifestation so it may begin its journey into a place of reality. Divinity, as Kether, in a state of awareness of ITSELF and having found the means to polarize (Chokmah and Binah) and create something more from ITSELF, yearns for manifest expression (Malkuth). And, once having manifested, yearns for the natural return to ITSELF. It is from the place of Chesed that this cycle takes root and foundation.

Chesed is the foundation upon which all creative effort begins its journey into being. It is the receptacle of the outpourings of the Supernal Triangle above the abyss (Da'At). This outpouring is the combined essence of the One (Kether), now polarized, becoming two and expressed through Chokmah (Wisdom) and Binah (Understanding).

The sphere of Chesed is one of abundance, obedience to the spiritual laws, authority and foundation. The extreme nature of its polar sphere Geburah, has now been brought to a place of greater insight regarding the necessity of final release in order to move forward. The point of focus and discomfort that arose in Geburah has now expanded to a place of truly seeing and experiencing the greater whole (larger picture) and the importance of having both a strong container to hold (Geburah) the outpour and a continual flow of expansive energy (Chesed) to draw it down into a place of manifest use (Malkuth).

The energy of Chesed acknowledges and accepts the limitless potential that arises when true abundance is embraced. Within this acceptance is also the potential of acting upon and creating more fully from what insight has been acquired through the energy and experiences of the previous spheres on the ascent up the Tree. These lessons and insights have now reached a place where they may be refined, adapted and molded to be more closely in accord with Divine Will versus the desires of ego.

Chesed is the place of cosmic memory. It is the refined aspect of Yesod (the storehouse of images and records) having been filtered, synthesized and finalized by the spheres acting upon the Yesodic energy in the ascent towards Chesed. Having arrived at this state of full access to memory of the aeons and creation itself, work may begin towards incorporating and using that memory where choice and Free Will are called to action. Chesed teaches and demands obedience to the laws of nature and the cosmic laws that is without question because the ego has been put aside and the workings of the Inner Divine have been activated. There is a gnosis or knowing that all will be and is as it should be, so there is no need to question, as there are no personal agendas.

The Settled Consciousness

The energy of Chesed is one of Consciousness that has received informed and generative spiritual powers from the Supernals and thus in turn emanates these in an expansive nature towards those Sephiroth that follow in order. In this state of being, consciousness has transcended beyond simple awareness of its Higher nature to awareness of how and where the point of origin of that Higher nature has evolved. It has in a way settled into the natural order and state of things and is at one with all, seeing itself part of all.

The Receptive Intelligence

Chesed is considered the Receptive Intelligence. In this way its energy is directed towards the point of receiving the Supernal energies of Binah/Chokmah and Kether and forming the ideology of these spheres in a way that is more easily understood as it is brought down towards manifestation. Its nature is that of having deep gnosis, founded upon the stability of higher purpose and then willingly releasing that energy for further refinement in its companion sphere of Geburah.

The Element of the Sphere

Water

Chesed is assigned the element of water, and in making use of this watery nature healing, deep insight and an infinite "sea" of possibilities opens to the seeker in revelation of the greater purpose. These are the waters that have been quickened within the womb of Binah is its downpour towards Chesed. These are the electrified waters that have been infused with unconditional love and are in receipt of the fires of the Cosmos from Chokmah. These are the waters of inspiration and depth of intuitive nature that guides the course of those who choose to cross the perilous Abyss of Da'at.

Numerical Value

Chesed is the **Fourth** Sphere. Within the energy of the number **4** is the basis of foundation, solidity of form and function and endurance or permanence. Four indicates change (as in the four seasons), versatility (as in the four elements) and a nice solid equi-sided base upon which to build from those changes a versatile nature of enduring qualities. Four also relates to the planet Mercury; the planet of communication. The essence of the fourth sphere, Chesed, is the ultimate form of communication and then dissemination of that synthesized communication through the vehicle of compassion, mercy and grace.

Location on the Tree

As we move up the Tree the energy of the spheres becomes more intense. Simultaneously, these energies also become less dense and more refined, with higher vibratory frequency. Because of the higher vibratory frequency it becomes paramount that each sphere work in tandem with its opposite. The distinction between each sphere is magnetically drawn towards the center point of balance (the Middle Way or Pillar of Equilibrium), with the polarized energy of each depending upon the other for full expression, thus force and form must work cohesively.

The Middle Sphere on the Pillar of Mercy

Placed at the center of the Middle Pillar of Mercy, Chesed receives the downpour from Chokmah and the upward striving of Netzach's energy. If we equate Chokmah with wisdom and Netzach with victory, Chesed becomes the central activator that takes in both streams of emanation, transforms them through its action of cohesion and causes the necessary expansion based on memory of all potential outcomes to create a deeper expression of Love informed by Divine wisdom.

CHOKMAH

The Divine Essence
and Knowledge of LOVE

CHESED

The mid-point of
the Pillar

Loving Kindness imbued with
and obedient to the Divine

NETZACH

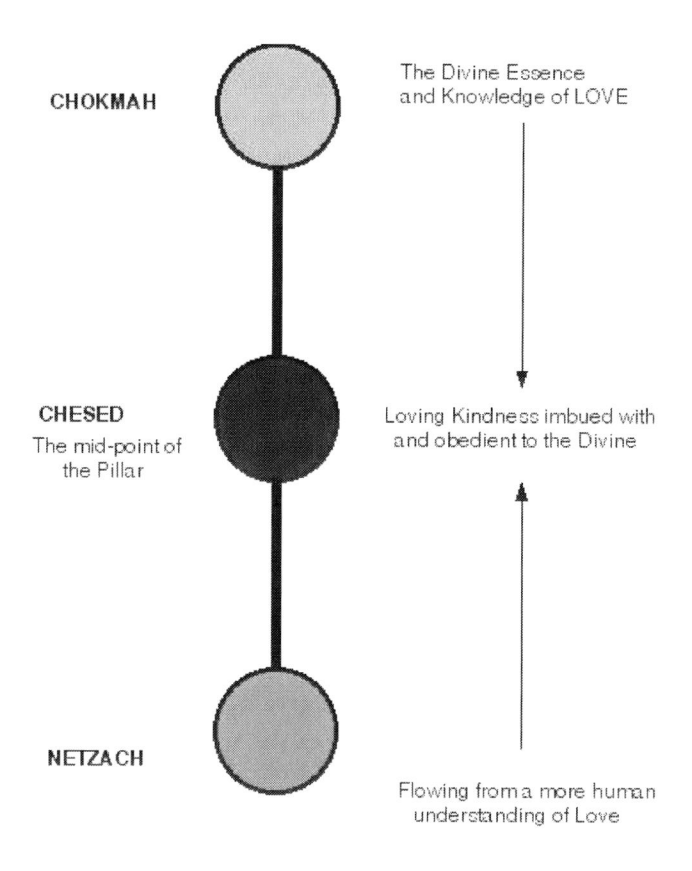

Flowing from a more human
understanding of Love

The Pillar of Mercy

Fig. 24

The Gateway to the Supernals

Chesed is the last sphere on ascending the Tree before stepping into the realm of the Supernals of Binah, Chokmah and Kether. It is the place of final choice that has been informed by the energy of the spheres below it and the decision to brave crossing the Abyss to reach the womb of the Great Mother (Binah). It is the Gateway to both Understanding (Binah) and Wisdom (Chokmah). Conversely, Chesed is also the natural outcome of the directed energy of these Supernals.

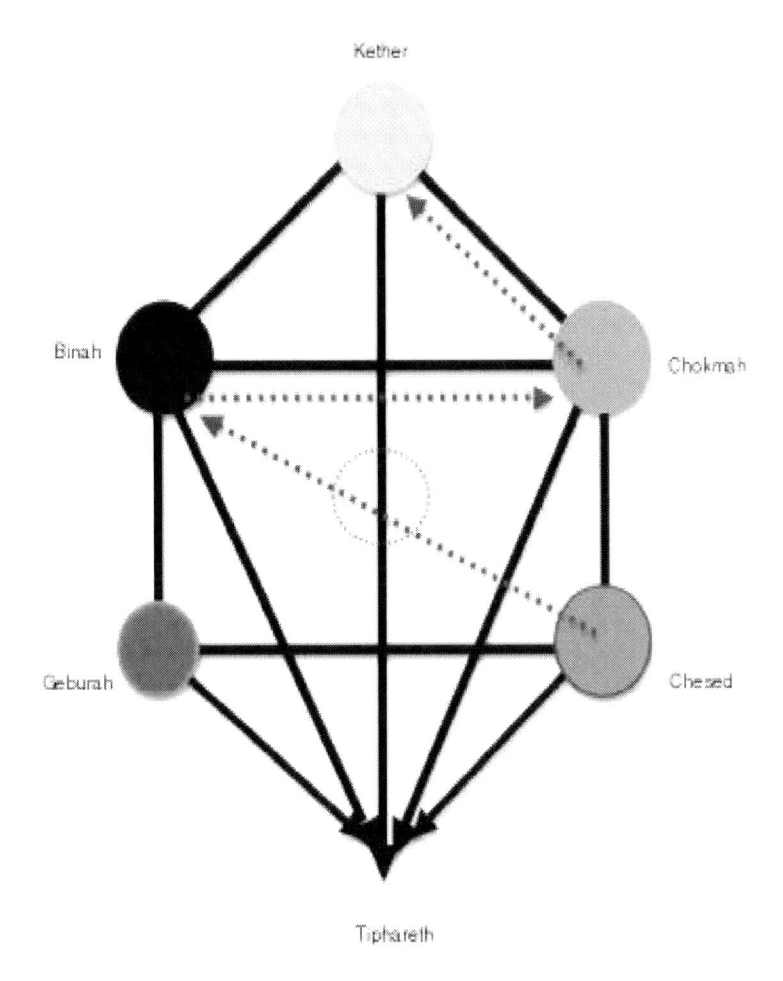

Fig. 25

The Womb of Manifestation

On descending the Tree, the sphere of Chesed, having received the emanations of Wisdom and Understanding stands as the first sphere of actuality and potential towards reality.

The illustration on the next page *(Fig. 26)* is my perception of this combined effort of creation. This collaborative thrust of energy is where potential of pure intent moves through Force (Chesed) to create the resultant Form (Geburah).

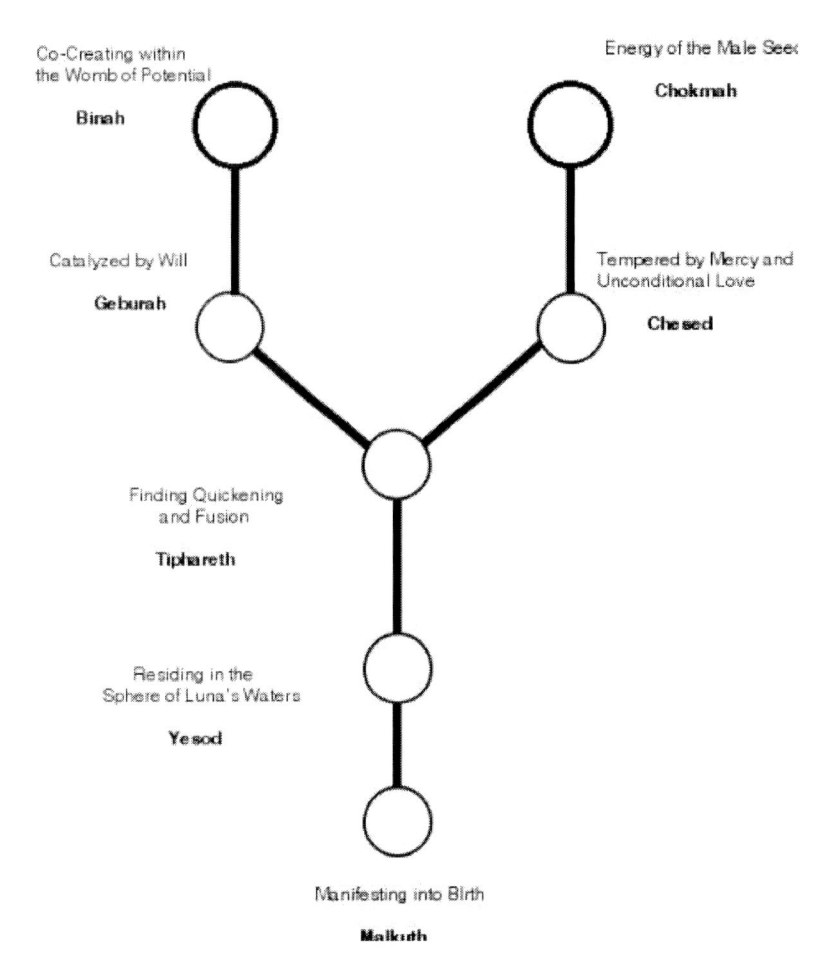

[Diagram: Tree of Life with sephiroth labeled:
- Binah — Co-Creating within the Womb of Potential
- Chokmah — Energy of the Male Seed
- Geburah — Catalyzed by Will
- Chesed — Tempered by Mercy and Unconditional Love
- Tiphareth — Finding Quickening and Fusion
- Yesod — Residing in the Sphere of Luna's Waters
- Malkuth — Manifesting into Birth]

Fig. 26

The Square of Foundation

In Chapter Six, we looked at the Energetic Triad (*Fig. 23*) as a square of foundation through the energies of Geburah and assignment of those spheres contained to a specific element.

To review, we noted that, if we look at any of the three connecting points in Figure 23 as we move around the perimeter of the square there is a pattern that emerges. The pattern is that of FIRE, WATER and AIR. This triad, or triangle represent the three points of flow and return that form the basis for energetic fire. This thought process is particularly useful if you engage in a regular energetic practice to enliven the spiritual fires within. In each case one of the elements acts as the positive point from which the initializing effects proceed. There is a moment of neutrality or pause where the initial charge is synthesized, transformed and reversed for the outpour or flow towards the point of negative magnetic polarity. The action of positive and negative reacting and acting upon one another creates the electric burst or fire that produces energy.

If we add the deeper insight of Geburic energy, the foundation of the 4 elements plus Spirit residing as the mid-point is created. If we look at this same square of foundation from the perspective of Chesed and its energetic nature, we can take this concept a step further with those elemental energies and apply them in a more expansive way. It may appear that the elements of association have shifted and are incorrect in some way, but if we take a closer look at the nature of the spheres, there is some logic to this.

Geburah
Will/Creation
Fire

Chesed
Memory
Earth

Tiphareth
Spirit

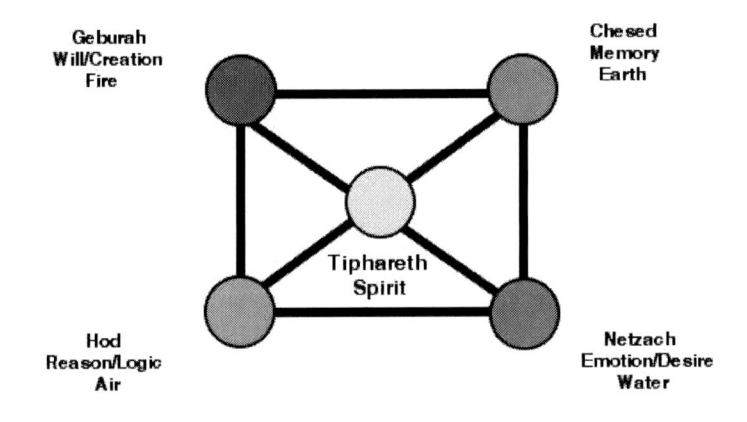

Hod
Reason/Logic
Air

Netzach
Emotion/Desire
Water

Fig. 27

- **Geburah still stands in the place of Fire and will, but the three other spheres take on another elemental attribute.**

- **Hod becomes the sphere of Air, inspiration that has been catalyzed and electrified by Geburah through the waters (its natural state) of its domain to provide the necessary charge that will issue forth light, idea and illumination.**
- **Netzach becomes the sphere of Water; its yearning for beauty, love and desire transformed through the fires (its natural state) of its domain to a place of flow and outpour and movement.**
- **Chesed becomes the sphere of Earth, the foundation and stable fertile grounds upon which all creative flow can be stabilized. It rises from the waters (its natural state) issued forth from the primal womb of the Great Mother (Binah).**
- **And, Tiphareth standing in the center as both receiver and distributor is the place of Spirit, the ultimate refinement at this level of creation of all that flows in and through it as moves as informed mind (air, its natural state).**

Movement from HOD

When we move diagonally from the place of Hod through the energy of Tiphareth and arrive at Chesed, we have taken pure logic, thought and reasoning and moved this idea through the filtering lens of Tiphareth; resulting with emanation into Chesed, a place of loving temperance. The interaction between the three is one of natural evolution as the Higher Self emerges as the primary point of communication between mind and action and is the natural outcome of that mind working in collaboration with Divine Will.

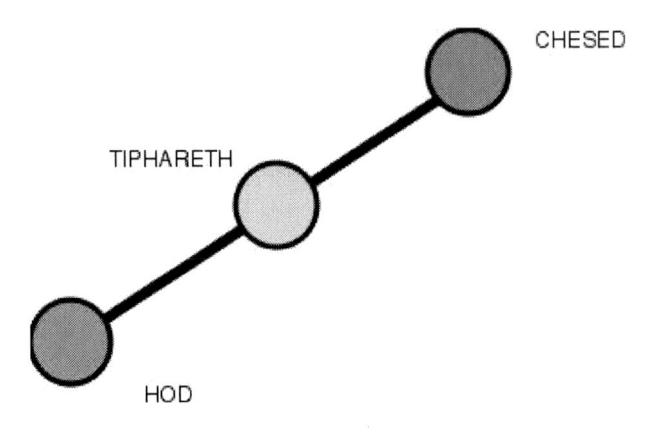

Fig. 28

The Spiritual Experience
The Vision of Love

The spiritual experience of Chesed is that of LOVE expressed in its Highest Form. This is considered the Sphere of Saints and the Hall of Masters or those who have ascended to their highest state of being and choose to remain on the Wheel of Incarnation to aid humanity. This energy, having claimed the mantle of power in Geburah, is power that is carried forward to a new state of being. It is now infused with authority and mastery over the baser nature and becomes the expression of unlimited compassion and unconditional Love of a Higher Order guided by the merciful Divine.

The Illusion of the Sphere
Bigotry, Hypocrisy, Tyranny

History holds the lesson of Chesed in its illusory state. The once beneficent ruler who, after having achieved an expansive state of power, becomes the tyrannical despot. Authority, control and power are all very seductive energies, and ones which the human ego feeds strongly from if not held in check. When the natural state of Chesed is driven from a place of human will those things that would be seen from a more open and broader view begin to take on the narrow gaze that moves towards exclusion and elitism. Bigotry against one or another group, that is ironically all part of that larger perspective, becomes the survival mechanism that is put into place to preserve one's authority and power. Of course, this authority and power are humanly ordained rather than achieved through Divine inspiration.

At this level of being, what should be of pure intent becomes a travesty of hypocritical display, sought in final desperation as the false foundations lay in ruin.

The Briatic Color
Blue

When we see the color Blue we usually respond in a relaxing gentle way. Blue has long been associated with healing. If we think of the color blue in nature, the sky and the oceans, each hold a mystery of their own. Each is expansive and infinite in quality and each holds within its nature the necessary components for survival; air/breath and water/moisture. The Briatic color of Chesed holds the memory of these mysteries. The sky contains the currents of air which reflect the fire and heat of the Sun. All embrace the earth that holds the ocean's waters, which hold the molecules of air warmed by the sun with its fluids. Air, Fire, Water and Earth; each of the elements of foundation are thus contained within the simple vibration of Chesed's Briatic color.

The Magickal Image
"A Mighty Crowned and Throned King"

The image that is attributed to the sphere of Chesed is that of a mighty king, wearing the crown of authority and seated on a throne of royalty. King Solomon and the Emperor Key of the tarot are apt representations of this image. True authority emanates from a place of great wisdom, much experience and a sense of the "right" balance and natural order of things. If a ruler is considered just and fair these attributes are enhanced and each decision arrived upon or order decreed comes from a place of wanting the best for all concerned. The warning here, however, is that the "best" is not always the desired or favorable outcome that would be most coveted. The "best" could be considered negative in all aspects; and this is where experience and having the broader scope in mind come into play. When we are able to step into the place of the merciful loving King, we are able to acknowledge that there will always be disparity between what is perceived as favorable and beneficial and harsh and cruel. Being able to distinguish, and more importantly, to accept this knowledge is the first step towards stepping into a place of Divinely inspired authority or the energy of the Mighty Crowned King sitting upon his justly deserved Throne.

Expression Through The Four Worlds

Atziluth - the Creative Urge

The Supreme Lord of Life

Gods/Goddesses of Authority

Osiris - Zeus - The Dagda

In the sphere of Chesed, Atziluth is exemplified in the archetypical energy of those Deities who exemplify the merit of sacrifice to achieve right action and the merciful splendor of bestowing the fruits of these labors upon humanity. These Deity act as the guiding Rays of Light towards the Divine and remind us of our spiritual nature that is contained in this incarnation within manifest form. Each of these Deity has the potential, authority and capacity for cruelty and destruction, but each has mastered the necessary control that can be giving and merciful in what is provided. On descent from the Supernals, the Deities within Chesed are a reminder that Mercy is always the conduit that is first attained from the Divine Source. The dismantling of that Mercy that is seen as the energy flows to Geburah is necessary for ultimate manifestation, but is not the original source of intent. On ascent towards Kether, the authority wielded by the Deity of Chesed is the final stopgap or testing place of pure intent, before one may stand the test of faith in Da'at and return to a natural state of Divinity. These God forms provide hope to humanity and inspire the desire for re-absorption of SELF through Binah and Chokmah and final return to the ONE of Kether, and it is through the beneficence of their Grace that one may aspire to Kingship.

Briah - Creation of a Concept - Archangel

Archangel Tzadkiel

"The Righteous of God"

The Archangel Tzadkiel is called " The Righteous of God". It is his province that deems that a state of "right" and "correctness" has been achieved once all the previous trials and tests have been faced and successfully navigated. He acts as the higher conscience of man; the man/woman who does what is right and necessary because there is nothing else that the individual can do. This is the only vision that is seen and it is no longer tainted or skewed by those energies that would produce haphazard correct action. The course is solidly planned and firmly bound by all the Laws to which it may be subject and all is in accord and a state of abundance.

Tzadkiel is the angel of judgment who urges us on towards this foundation of right action. He is the holder of what we only fleetingly know as our best nature. It is his job to remind us as we move through our mundane lives of what that best or Divine nature is. His is the voice that whispers in your ear when an action is not in keeping with that Divine nature and his is the seed of thought in our minds that calls us forth from our daily slumber when we become sated by illusory wealth and greed.

Yetzirah - Forming the Image of the Concept

Angels - Chasmalim
" The Brilliant Ones"

This angelic vision of the Chasmalim was written of in the Bible, Ezekiel 1:4, where he talks about the beings "enveloped in brightness and which gleamed like electrum" (ChShML). The figures into which this cloud of the Chasmalim then proceeded to manifest in this vision are the same as those pictured in the Tarot Key X: The Wheel of Fortune of The Four Holy Creatures:

The Winged Bull, The Winged Lion, The Eagle and The Winged Man

The Chasmalim direct the focus of Archangel Tzadkiel's call to "conscience" in a manner that will be both productive and beneficial. They are regarded as those who act to bring cohesion and balance to that which has been torn apart and reformed. They are the Angels of fusion and provide the fires that act in a manner of cauterizing what needs to be healed from the act of excision that occurred at Geburah. In this way they are also considered the restorers of order and work in conjunction with the Seraphim (Fiery Avenging angels of Geburah) of Geburah to light the way for new found balance amidst the chaotic outpour at the level of Geburah.

Within the jovial expanse of Chesed, the Chasmalim are the keepers of cosmic joy and bliss. They are the warm feeling that produces the smile of contentment and the energetic heat that is acquired by a good laugh and state of relaxation and calm.

Assiah - The World of Expression - Planetary
Jupiter/Jove
King of the Gods

In the semantics of Astrology, Jupiter is the planet of Expansion. Its symbol represents the crescent of receptivity waxing as a focus of material activity. It is also noted as one of the brightest planets in the sky. Its radiance spreading far and wide and illuminating all in its path.

The expression of Jupiterian energy in Chesed is about reaping the abundance of flow and expansion by rising ABOVE the glamour and seduction of the overwhelming experience of unrestricted receipt. It brings the lesson of learning the control of Power (through Geburah's actions) before the use of power may be claimed. There is an abundance of goodwill that can be achieved through this application of restraint in the taking and asking of only the amount that is justifiably needed, and then passing on what is left in excess to others in greater need.

In this place of expression, we are able to enjoy the rewards of right action we have attracted to ourselves, and in so doing provide the model for others to follow suit.

The Living Tree: Personal Study

Opening to Judgment

This set of exercises is intended to make you more aware of the varied choices and opportunities for right action that are presented daily to those standing within the mantle of Power.

Active Engagement

In the last study we used the energy of Geburah filtered through the energy of Tiphareth to give thought to the events in the news.

Follow the news for the next three weeks. Identify the Geburic events. How could they be "Tipharized"?

For the next two weeks, look again at several events in the news. See where those events may have been averted or had different outcome had they been filtered through the lens of Chesed. How much attention was given to seeing the "complete and broader" picture? How many different perspectives do you think were offered in reaching the final determination? What different or similar choices would you have made?

Chapter Eight

BINAH

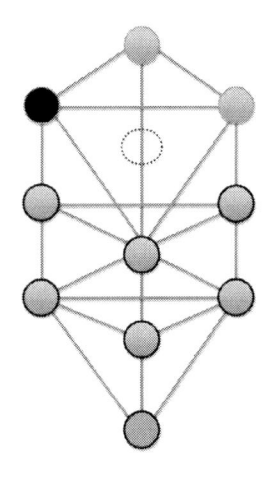

UNDERSTANDING

The Great mother
Sighs and oceans
Tremble and swell
Filled with her breath.

The Bright mother
Opens her eyes
Gazing with expectation
And the world is suddenly
Ablaze with illumined gaze.

The Dark mother
Stretches out her hand
And you are left
Exposed and vulnerable

Your darkest secrets
Laid bare.

The Creatrix moves
And life awakens
As the fabric of form
Is woven gently within
The folds of her embrace.

The Lesson of the Sphere

Keywords

Supreme Mother/Creatrix

Archetypal womb through which all life is made manifest

(Malkuth)

The Intuitive SELF

Feminine Principle

Primal Form and Timeless Void

Foundation/Stability of Upper Triad

The Energy of the Sphere

Having crossed the Abyss of Da'at, there is now a distinct and clear separation between the Supernals of Kether, Chokmah and Binah and all that lay below them. The Supernals are the creators of what is given form, essence, personality and life in the subsequent spheres below it. The final outpouring resulting in Malkuth and physical manifest form.

Binah is the sphere of restriction; contraction and the confinement of the flood of force and flow that had previously emanated via

Chokmah from the primary state of Kether. It is the "will to form" and the creative vessel that holds the Divine Spark in preparation for its eventual initiatory experience of birth.

Within the energy of Binah we find the Mother and Divine Creatrix; who contains within herself the archetypal womb through which all life is made manifest (Malkuth). It is the nature of the male to provide the seed of life, but it is the feminine principle that gives it life, provides the space for gestation and ultimately releases the manifest form into existence or being. It is that feminine principle that holds the primal form within the womb that is both void and full. The vessel that holds nothing also provides the space and potential for it to be filled. This dynamic of the Divine feminine is expressed in its triune nature as **MARAH, AIMAH** and **AMA.**

Marah - Of the Sea

Binah in this form is the aspect of the primordial waters which contain all of life in its formless state of potentiality. This is the space of the Intuitive SELF. Within this fluidity is the knowledge of complete understanding and gnosis of the properties and generative qualities of force being acted upon by the temporary limitation of form. Even the great oceans have boundaries of shoreline to prevent the overtaking of a formless substance as well as to create the container within which sea life may thrive.

Another concept that often arises in conceptualization of this primal soup is the utter silence that is held. This is the powerful Silence that is deafening and overwhelming. The silence before life comes into being. The silence that holds the space within which manifestation may be quickened and brought to fruition. This is the Silence that is spoken of regarding magickal and mystical work. To Be Silent is to invite action and receptivity.

Aimah - Fertile/Light Mother

The Bright Mother is the giver of life. She is the ground that teems with the proper balance of nutrients that will produce the most bountiful of harvest. This is the energy of Binah when her fertility of creative effort is at its prime point. Flush and full from the force of flow from Chokmah and through the dynamic charge of Light giving way to matter, progeny is raised from the primal waters and issues forth into the care of the Dark Mother.

Ama - The Dark Mother/Crone

The Dark Mother is the restrictive nature of Binah. She is, when necessary, the destroyer of the Life the Bright mother has bestowed. All endeavors do not go as planned, just as all life is not always viable. In the facet of AMA, Binah becomes the selective creator. Issuing forth enough so that a choice and selection can be made from the strongest forms that hold the most potential for eventual outcome. She represents the empty womb awaiting revitalization; but holding onto the expressive charge of Life.

Another title often given in connection with Binah and the Feminine principle is:

Khorsia - The Throne

Another of the titles of Binah is Khorsia, or Throne, and the image is that of Binah as the provider of the framework upon which Malkuth is built. She is called the Throne of Wisdom, because she is the support and structure needed for the Wisdom of Chokmah to emanate from. This is the concept of an interchange between Chokmah (The Force) and Binah (The Word or breath of Creation and attribution to the Throat chakra); this Force being continual and enduring as it responds to the nature of time (Saturn).

In this place Binah is also the authority who defines how and what that form will take. It is through the skill of her vision and understanding of the entire workings of Creation that the appropriate amount of restriction is doled out to become the container for creative expression.

The Sanctified Consciousness

The energy of Binah is one of Consciousness that understands the concepts that have gone into the creation of all manner of things. This is the consciousness that is the Church that holds the life of the church; the Temple that contains the essence of the beliefs and foundations of that belief; the Holy of Holies and the force that has consecrated and has raised the sacred energy to a place of sacredness. Binah is the origin of the form of the idea of consciousness and as such is the essence of that form as well as a state of that consciousness.

The Rational Intelligence

Binah is considered the Rational Intelligence. The word "Binah" means "Intelligence" in Hebrew. This meaning does not refer to the intelligence of our subjective intellect, but rather to the authentic intelligence, intuition, and enlightenment of consciousness. Ascending the tree, Binah sits at the highest pinnacle of pure Reason (Hod) filtered and refined through Geburah and expressed in its "essence or root" having arrived at Binah. Her energy is the highest level of mental expression; incomprehensible and inscrutable in its expression.

The Element of the Sphere
Root of Water (Water of Water)

Binah is assigned the element of **Root of Water**. Each of the elements has the attribute of containing essences of the other three elements contained within and being reflected in varying degrees in accord with their power of exertion. In keeping with this thought, water is expressed as Air of Water, Fire of Water, Earth of Water and in its most pure essence Water of Water. The three Supernal spheres of Binah, Chokmah and Kether are all ascribed the pure essence of the element they represent, as they themselves are of the Highest and most refined nature of all the sephiroth of the Tree.

The sphere of Binah holds the space of the primordial waters from which all of creation was birthed. It was the within the purest form of the element of water that Life was enlivened. This Divine birthing could only be achieved in the most refined and rarified state of elemental essence; the summation of all emotional urge folded in upon itself from the spring of pure source. The pure expression of the intuitive nature that is both creator and receiver of this Divine communication; and the heart of hearts that released upon the path of manifestation becomes the waters that heal, consume and transform.

Numerical Value

Binah is the **Third** Sphere on the Tree of Life. Within the energy of the number **3** is the structure of harmony and the triune nature that forms the three-sided triangle of fire, action and will. At the level of the supernals, all flows in harmony; each path, each sphere working in tandem with one another in the creative effort. Additionally, each component offers a different perspective or dynamic to contribute to that outpour. Three faces, each in support of the other yet one in the same and emanating from the One.

Location on the Tree

The Pinnacle Sphere on the Pillar of Severity

Through the Root of Water (Binah) the Directive Energy of the Root of Fire (Chokmah) moves to a place of discharge within the organizing, lawful movement of the Root of Air (Kether) in the space of Aether (The Three Veils-Ayin-Ayin Soph and Ayin Soph Aur)

BINAH — The Divine Essence and Understanding of Creative Form

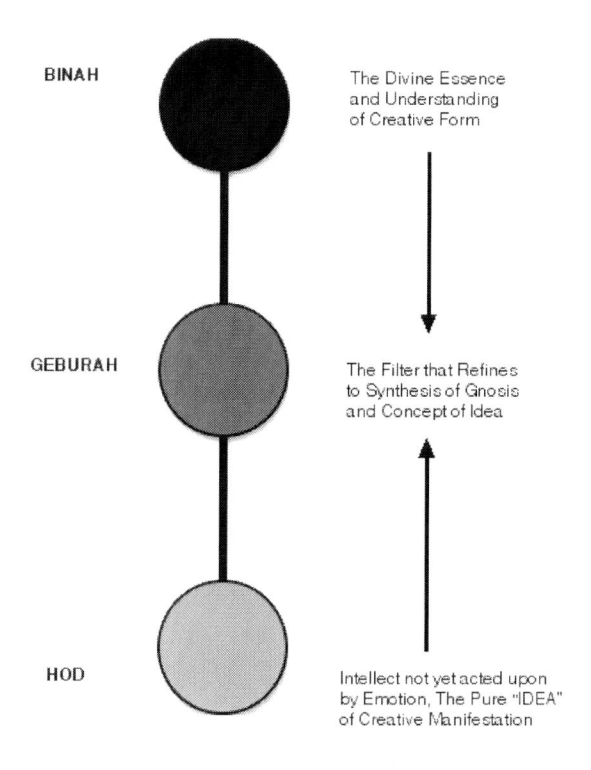

GEBURAH — The Filter that Refines to Synthesis of Gnosis and Concept of Idea

HOD — Intellect not yet acted upon by Emotion, The Pure "IDEA" of Creative Manifestation

Fig. 29

The Fire of the Supernals

The Briatic Colors of the Supernal spheres tell the story of creative movement from the brilliance of the pure light of Kether to the synthesis of light and dark reflected in the grey of Chokmah and infused with greater definition within the black density of form contained in Binah. The colors of the spheres below these three are infused with vibration that gives more vibrancy and differentiation of color- blue, red, yellow, green, orange, violet and the earth tones of Malkuth. Although the values of Kether, Chokmah and Binah may not be the typical thought of Fire, the underlying current of brilliance of Light (blinding in its nature) and its disbursement through the polarized darkness of Chokmah and Binah is the first Fire of Divine Light in its primal state of catalytic creation.

Force and Form Must Work Cohesively

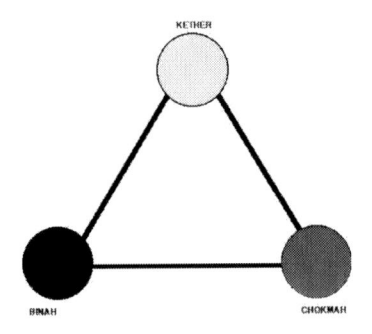

Fig. 30

Just as Chesed is the Gateway to both Wisdom (Chokmah) and Understanding (Binah), once having crossed this threshold through Da'at and approaching Binah, the realm of Pure Spirit has been entered. Binah provides a place of Foundation/Stability and being connected to Chokmah via a Path, the two interact together balancing these highly refined energies in readiness for reunion at the Source point of KETHER.

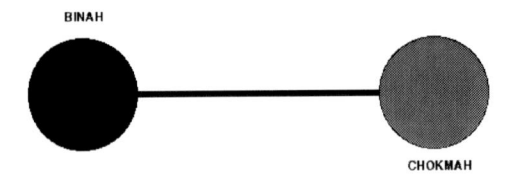

Fig. 31

The Womb of Manifestation

In Chapter Seven we discussed the womb of manifestation through the energies of Chesed. Now in looking at this diagram again, we can continue the path of thought upwards towards Binah. Da'at sits in the place centrally, hidden and similar in nature to the womb itself. Its mystery and the actual goings on that infuse the spark of life may be revealed to some degree in the scientific studies, but the true spiritual essence and nature of the quickening are not something committed to an ultrasound or thesis paper. This force remains hidden within the pulse of potential. This is the first place of that force being held in the restrictive nature of form as the Divine Spark moves into the life of manifestation downwards towards Malkuth.

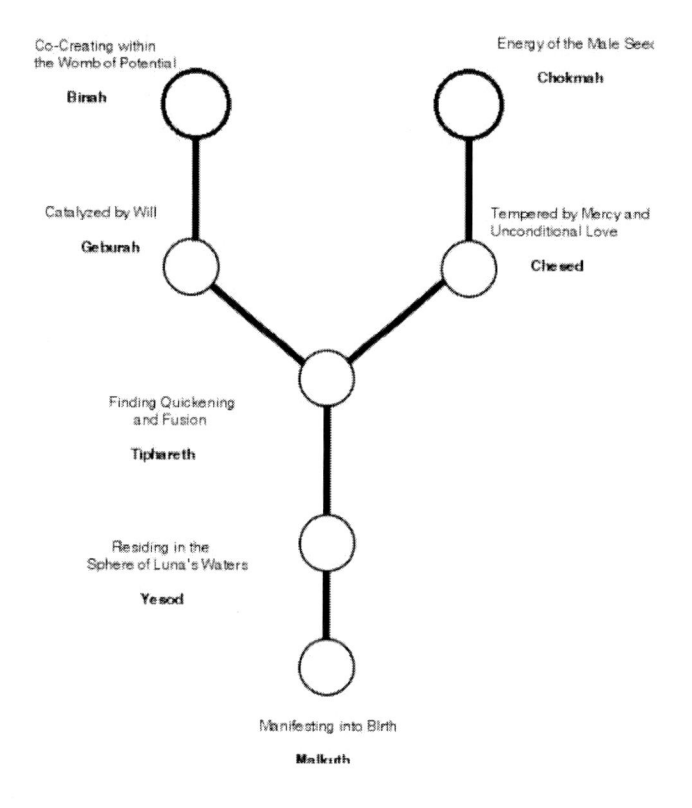

Fig. 32

The Spiritual Experience

The Vision of Sorrow

The spiritual experience of Binah is that of Sorrow. Sorrow having been borne from the deep underlying understanding of the greater principles and concepts that are part of the evolutionary process of creating manifest form. It could be considered the worrisome foreboding that is experienced by the mother as each child leaves the protection and guidance of her wisdom to venture forth into the world. Because the mother has knowledge and understanding of what that transition may hold in future events, there is a deep sorrow as well as joy that her beloved child will endure the trials and tribulations of becoming self-sufficient, independent and an individualized being. This is the sorrow of the Great Mother for all the seeds of life she will initialize and set forth towards individual form.

The Illusion of the Sphere

Death

The illusion of Binah is that of Death, finite and complete. This would be the natural vice of this sphere as there is so much life and birth contained within her. For those who do not see the cyclic nature of the mysteries; death is the final chapter. But if you probe deeper you will find that within the decayed body of the lifeless, other forms of life thrive and continue on. All that returns to the Mother, whether it be the Mother Earth, The Cosmic Mother or the human Mother returns to a state of rebirth, nurture and new life. Death is at once the final and the beginning stage of all living matter; for in order that something new may burst forth, something must give way.

The Briatic Color

Black

Any artist will confirm that Black is not the absence of color but all the colors contained in a state waiting for light to be shone and reflected upon it. What happens when you shine a light across a seemingly black surface? You can easily see the blues, purples, deep reds, and more reflected in shimmering dots across that surface. These are the emanations of the other spheres that sit below the supernal of the Great Mother. And, within her all are contained and given life.

The Magickal Image

"A Mature Woman. A Matron "

An excellent example of the magickal image for Binah is that of an elderly woman sitting in a rocking chair. You can visualize her rocking back and forth as she reflects on her life's achievements, disappointments and perhaps even thinking about her loved ones and the children she may have nurtured. There is a regal quality in this image and great power that is both subtle and overwhelming at the emotional level.

This is the energy of the Crone, the wise woman who has lessons to teach and will not always do so in a loving manner because she has the wisdom of past experience as her guide. She knows that life is difficult, but within those difficulties lie the great opportunities for complete transformation and in this space of comfort, we may all embrace the mortality of our existence and welcome the embrace of the Great Mother.

Expression Through The Four Worlds

Atziluth - The Creative Urge

The Supreme Lord of Life

The Creatrix Goddesses

Isis - Nuit - Shakti

Within the sphere of Binah, Atziluth is exemplified in the archetypical energy of those Deities from whose being worlds are given the spark of life. These Goddesses are considered the Aloath Elohim or Mother of Mothers. They initialize the realization of the Higher Self and the potential for exchange and interchange between Lower and Higher SELF. They act as the mother who wants the best for her child and prods and urges that child towards its highest potential and eventual understanding of its own nature. Isis is the path of memory of wholeness and reassembling the parts to make the whole so that Osiris may transform all who pass through the Gates of the Underworld. Nuit is the body of the heavens that gives birth to all cosmic matter as Geb is the sustaining seed that is enlivened. And Shakti with her Lord Shiva in union is the fire and heat of the first Divine spark that enlivens the primordial waters towards creation from creation.

Briah - Creation of a Concept - Archangel

Archangel Tzaphkiel

"The Beholder of God"

The Archangel Tzaphkiel (not a typo and not to be confused with Tzadkiel of Chesed) is called " The Beholder of God". It is his province to observe and contemplate the Divinity of matter. It is through this channel that God and Man can observe one another. Tzaphkiel acts to focus the intent of scrutiny where it may be best used towards the realization of what the creator has created and what the creation sees of himself reflected through the force of that which created him.

Knowledge is gained through observation and action is upheld by knowing what that action will bring. Tzaphkiel looks from all perspectives, sees all and then forms that knowing into what may be transformed by Binah into deep understanding. To see the true face of God is to see the image of our Divine Selves and ultimately to bring that divinity to a place of understanding within our own being.

Yetzirah - Forming the Image of the Concept

Angels - Aralim

" The Thrones"

The Aralim are the angels of strength and stability. They are the necessary foundation upon which Binah can build. And, help the individual build, refine and form his/her own throne and temple of power within. It is through their efforts that one learns and masters authority over and of the self so that a higher form of this SELF may come to a place of selflessness. They are also the upholders of the containers through which the energy of Binah may move in a stabilized and controlled way.

Assiah - The World of Expression - Planetary

Saturn

Organization - Structure - Time

Saturn's function is that of contraction, and linear time is one of the greatest restrictors of natural flow. The Roman god Saturn is strongly influenced by the Greek God, Cronus. The word Cronus is related to "chronos" which means time. Saturn, astrologically, is the "Keeper of Time", and brings maturity, wisdom, and simplicity to people over time. It is human nature to be impatient and aware of time in a way that is not always productive. Developing "patience" in these matters opens an awareness of the infinite nature of things. It is with great patience and care that a mother nurtures and teaches her young, with the hopes that as time passes they will heed the lessons well and move forward through time in health, joy and growth.

Another term for Saturn is *Dweller on the Threshold*. Binah awaits at the end of the hidden path of Da'at and the Abyss. Whereas Jupiter and the Law of Mercy are the gateway of beginning before crossing the Abyss, Saturn stands in greeting at the Threshold of Binah upon entering the realm of the Supernals after the trials of Da'at. This is another of Saturn's many titles, duties and responsibilities in the unfolding of the Path. In this respect, the energies of Saturn are directly responsible in the "formation of faith". Faith that what awaits in crossing the threshold of initiation, death and rebirth is the return and awakening of the inner Divine.

Saturn is the planet of initiation. Of taking those lessons learned by way of other life time experiences or those of this lifetime and reforming them, restating them and then setting up the necessary limiting form to make us confront them head on. Every initiation is considered a death and rebirth of mind, body soul or way of life. This is the Saturn of Binah. This is the womb **before** rebirth/manifestation, the barrier that must be passed, and the challenge unrealized and incomplete. This is the struggle that teaches us the most about who we are and what our greater purpose is. What greater struggle is there then birth? The separation from that which is comfort, love, and careless blissful existence into the unknown and unknowable. It is taking the leap into the Light and knowing of the risk of obliteration by that light. This is the sorrow of Binah. Losing that which has been held closely within and knowing that you must ultimately urge it on towards its own place of creation.

The Living Tree: Personal Study

Opening to The Mother

This set of exercises is intended to make you more aware of the impact of holding onto those areas and things within our lives that are no longer productive and using the space of deeper insight to birth a new plan of action.

Journaling: Finding Your Place of Understanding

There are frequently times when we wish we had said or done something differently when confronted with a person or certain situation. These thoughts come in hindsight and many times, if we think more deeply on the situation, clues and other levels of understanding come to the front that were completely missed in the energy of the exact moment.

Reflecting on these additional bits of information may not change the outcome, but they do offer opportunities for a greater level of understanding, both about the nature of our response mechanisms and also about the person or situation that arose. Becoming aware of these energetic patterns, we can then choose to hold onto what is of productive nature and/or abandon those responses that are limiting and blinding to the truths being presented.

- Think back to an event or situation that recently occurred where the outcome was not as you wished. Write this experience down and make particular note of what you felt impacted this negative outcome.

- Now, seeing with the clarity and caring nature of Binah's right action, write down the information you wish you had been aware of that would have changed your response. Make a list of those things that if you had a deeper understanding of their nature would have either changed your opinion, or in thinking more deeply, would have caused you to give greater emphasis in a particular direction.

Chapter Nine

CHOKMAH

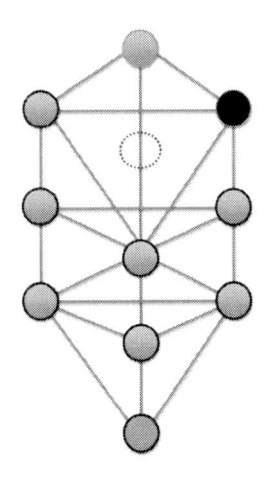

WISDOM

I sit in the reflection
Of His gaze
And rapture
Fills my being.

The swirlings of cosmos
And galaxy
Wind around me
Drawing my being
Into the vortex
Of formless unity.

He looks upward
And the light
Of a million stars
Pointedly glare back.
Each flowing into
Its own rhythm of
Celestial course.

He looks downward
And form moves
And stirs beneath
The scrutiny of HIS gaze
All is quickened by
This illumined SELF-awareness.

Formless brilliance flashes
Its point of beacon
Drawing HIS gaze
Upwards
And in response
The path is opened.

The singular eye of
The primal void
Focuses as
Droplets of soul filled
Tears issue forth.
This torrent of force
A floodgate
Of potentiality.

The Cosmic Father draws
This river into HIS Essence.
The Great Mother parts the veil
And readies her womb
As seed spills forth and
The circuit of creation
Fulfills its promise.

I sit in the reflection
Of HIS gaze and
Rapture fills my being
The quickening now
Complete and the first spark
Of Life lay sleeping in
My fertile belly.

The Lesson of the Sphere

Keywords

Sophia

Force

Stimulation

Potential

Objectiveness

The Energy of the Sphere

The sphere of Chokmah is the creative vessel, which holds the Divine Spark in preparation for its eventual initiatory experience of birth. Its holy name YHVH, the Tetragrammaton (*see Fig. 4)*, means, "to be". As the Root of Fire, Chokmah is the first sphere of desire towards greater expression. There is also objectivity and detachment in that desire. The goal is one of continued creation by the means that are necessary to ensure that. This is not questioned and remains in state of neutrality moving ever onwards in its natural sequence of events.

Within the energy of Chokmah we find the Father/Stimulator. His is the seed that ensures that the egg of potential will not remain inert and unviable. It is the nature of the male to provide the seed of life. Without this outpour, the feminine principle that gives it life and provides the space for gestation and release into a manifest form of existence (or being) would never occur. It is from this principle that the Wisdom of Chokmah is made evident. This is Wisdom of the cyclical and continued nature of energy, life and the Universe. It is pure unadulterated "knowing" that simply exists because it knows no other way "to be". In descent from

Kether, Wisdom is the first attribute of the great Divinity received by Chokmah. On ascent from the manifest plane of Malkuth, Wisdom is the last gift that is received and as such this all knowingness destroys the boundaries and limitations of the world, as we know it, including our perceived notions of ourselves. It is for this reason that in discussion of these Higher Supernals, metaphor and analogy that resonates and is comprehensible to us as human beings is all that can be used; for these are the spheres and energies that cannot be articulated or described in any manner that one in physical incarnation could comprehend. They are the ideals we are striving towards as translated into a human experience.

The energy of Chokmah is that of the archetypal Sage of all learning that extends into the furthest and most ancient reaches of the Universe. It is the experience of worlds before they were created as moved through its essence by the Source of those creations. Within the emanation of Kether into Chokmah and Binah, Chokmah stands as the Cosmic Father just as Binah holds the essence of the Great Mother. It is this need for polarity of energy that creates and separates into the two distinct energies we call Male and Female-Force and Form. But, as with all states of potentiality there is still within each of those spheres (Chokmah and Binah) the opposite polarity. In this way, Chokmah is also equated with the Greek Sophia or Spirit (Goddess) of wisdom. In this way the dynamic interplay between Force and Form, Male and Female, Chokmah and Binah is a necessity that must be initialized to complete the creative action that will be generated within the sphere of Kether.

In the Judeo-Christian tradition the goddess Sophia is seen as the initiator, the source of great wisdom, and keeper of the knowledge and wisdom of the mysteries. She is the holder of true Gnosis, and in the strength and care of that knowledge is the Divine Illuminator to shine forth for all who are held in the illusion of darkness and their lesser nature.

The Radiant Consciousness

The energy of Chokmah is one of Consciousness that radiates out the pure essence of consciousness in its primal state of illumined activity. Just as Binah is the origin of the form of the idea of consciousness and as such is the essence of that form as well as a state of that consciousness, Chokmah is the product of pure consciousness unrestricted and flowing freely from Creator to Creation. Its consciousness is not bound by time or space as it resides in all time and all space. It is in this way that true wisdom is reflected. A state of being that encompasses all and holds the key to the manifest world waiting to be used in opening as it flows towards Binah.

The Illuminating Intelligence

Chokmah, standing in refection of Kether cannot be anything other than reflective of this Great Light that is the All. Its nature is that of the intelligence of Higher understanding, potential and creation because it has received firsthand the experience and wisdom of this point of separation. Chokmah is Action and impetus in its most pure aspect, not yet restricted and limited by the Formative and ordering energies of Binah.

The Element of the Sphere
Root of Fire (Fire of Fire)

Chokmah is assigned the element of **Root of Fire**. This is the Cosmic Fire of first creation that enlivened the Waters of Nun and gave rise to the spark of Life. The Root of Fire is that which acts as the fuel of the Divine Mind, burning away the residue of what would naturally delay individualization and cause inertia within the potential of expansion. This potential is the Flame of desire for union of polarity, union of will and reunion of flesh and Spirit, Soul and the Limitless All. These are the fires of Divine inspiration that once taken hold burn brightly and eternally in the Heart of the Seeker.

Numerical Value

Chokmah is the **Second** Sphere on the Tree of Life. Within the energy of the number **2**, is the affinity of collaboration. It is movement from a singular place to one of experiencing the energy of another. It can also be thought of in terms of sacrificing parts of oneself to make another and making space and container to hold that other thing while retaining that part which created it. It is awareness that there is something beyond yourself and the yearning and striving for creating another to act and be acted upon.

Location on the Tree

The First Seeds of Insemination

Chokmah sits at the top of the Pillar of Mercy. If we look at the energy of this pillar, we see the pattern of unconditional Love that flows from one sphere to the other. We see also the transformative quality that occurs when the simple and pure knowledge of love is acted upon through the experience of loving-kindness; drawing this transformed energy upwards towards gnosis of the Divine essence of Love. Chokmah, having directly received the outpourings of the source of the highest nature and principle of Love sees it only from the vantage point of pure energy striving to reach form in the manifest realm. It is these first viable seeds that when implanted within the womb of the Great Mother will grow and adapt to a form that offers hope and potential to all of life as it reaches upwards towards the source of its own life.

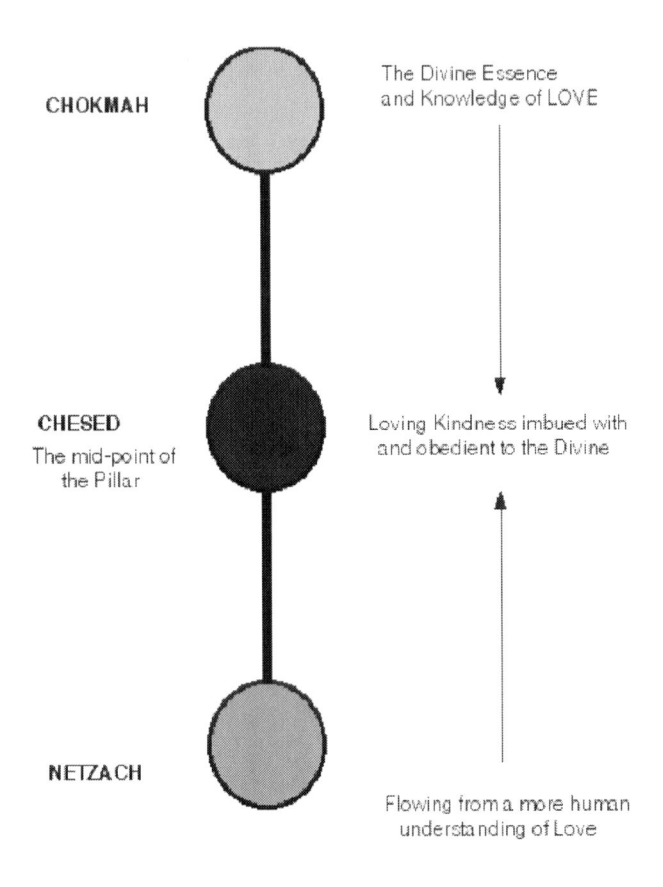

CHOKMAH — The Divine Essence and Knowledge of LOVE

CHESED
The mid-point of the Pillar — Loving Kindness imbued with and obedient to the Divine

NETZACH — Flowing from a more human understanding of Love

The Pillar of Mercy

Fig. 33

The Cosmic Couple

Without the form of Binah, the potential of Chokmah can descend no further. Too much energy or imbalance on either pillar would result in chaos; it is for this reason that we can think of Binah and Chokmah as the Supernal Mother and the Supernal Father. Each is drawing upon the other and the Universal flow of energy that created the Cosmos is the origin of their union. And, both sitting at the base of the Supernal Triangle gives each other the necessary energetic interaction and access to the direct path of their Source.

The Point of Destiny

KETHER

CHOKMAH

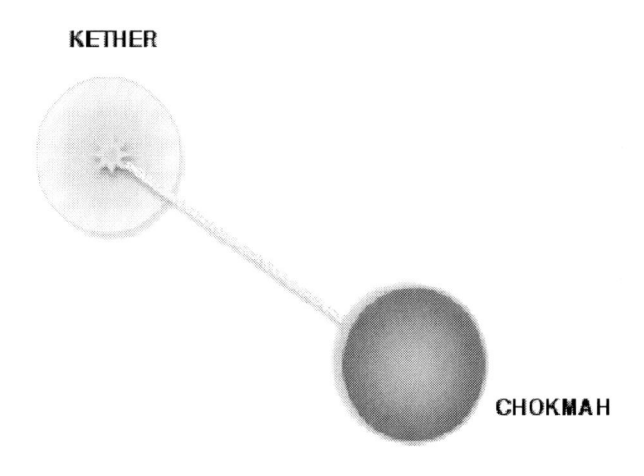

Fig. 34

The symbol of the straight line is attributed to the sphere of Chokmah. In order to make sense of this we must also include the energy of emanation from Kether. According to mathematical theory a "point" is a marker of place but in and of itself has no dimension. If, however, that point extended into space it becomes a straight line. If we think of Kether as the point of space within the void of formlessness, its emanation outward towards Chokmah extends the point of itself to become a straight line that acts upon and emanates the flow of formless force into Chokmah.

Womb of Manifestation

In the consideration of the pure state of the energies of Binah and Chokmah we now have the polarized form necessary for creative outpour from the Godhead of Kether. The negative and positive, the feminine and masculine. And, within their union and awareness of each other's dynamic pulse of force and form, the cosmic womb is ready to be synthesized and quickened.

KETHER

Co-Creating within the Womb of Potential
Binah

Energy of the Male Seed
Chokmah

Catalyzed by Will
Geburah

Tempered by Mercy and Unconditional Love
Chesed

Finding Quickening and Fusion
Tiphareth

Residing in the Sphere of Luna's Waters
Yesod

Manifesting into Birth
Malkuth

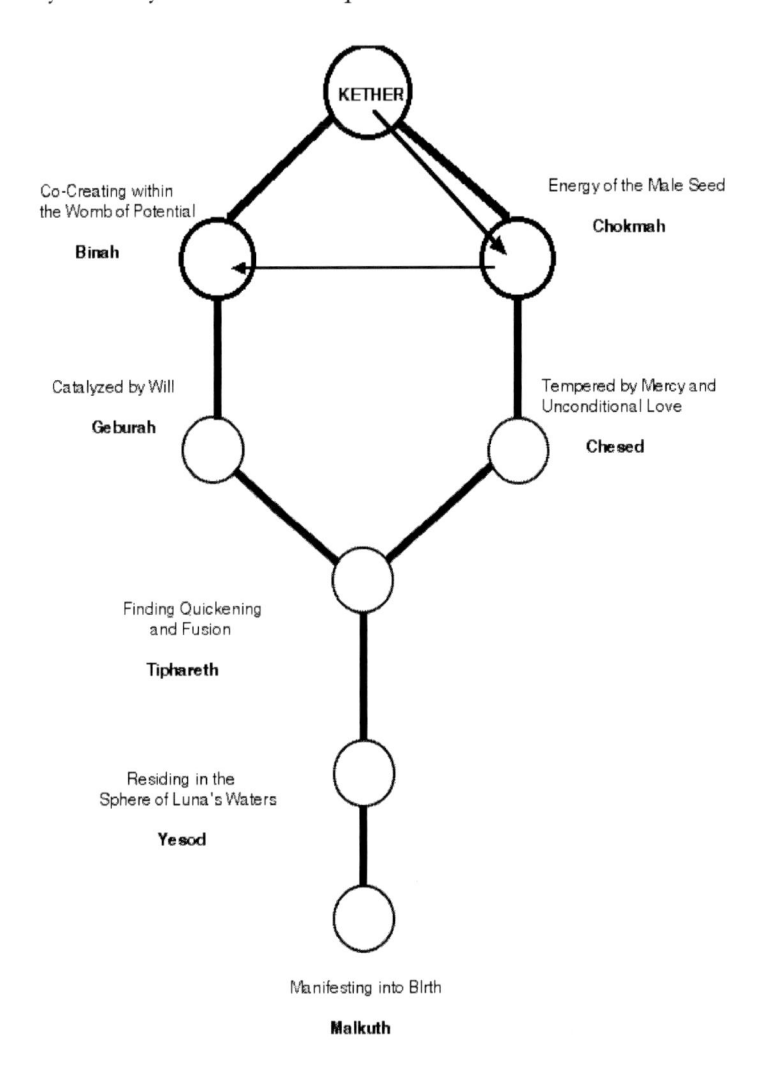

Fig. 35

We return once again to the womb of manifestation now seeing it through the vision of Chokmah; the first initiator of the final form. It is the dynamic interaction between Binah and Chokmah that allows for the downward thrust towards manifest form.

Without the seed of Chokmah, Binah would be inert. Additionally we can see the energy of the Godhead of Kether looking downward towards its final emanation in the place of Malkuth.

The Manifest Flow

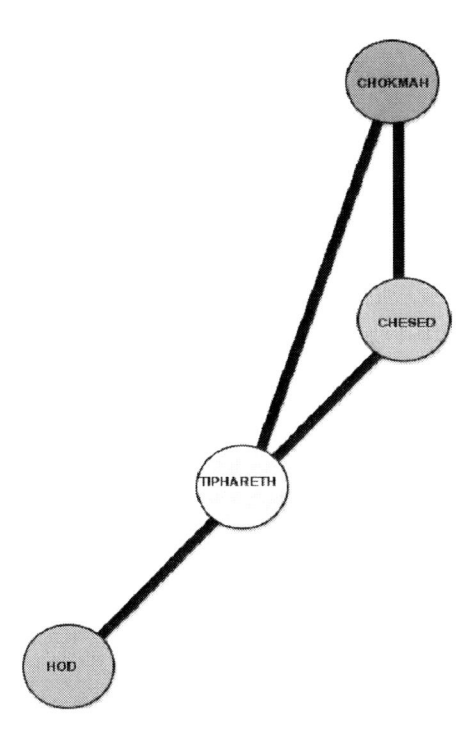

Fig. 36

If we follow the Path from Hod to Tiphareth we see how thought and intellect is transformed and filtered through the sphere of Beauty. We continue to move that energy following the Path from Tiphareth to Chokmah and we can better understand the essence of the Higher vibration of wisdom versus the more manifest of intellect/knowledge. And, finally Chesed stands in the place of the outer point of the Triangle formed between Tiphareth and Chokmah. The energy of this path being one of illumined energy (Tiphareth) flowing through the expanse of the wisdom of the Laws of the Universe (Chokmah) pouring down to manifest Informed and right action in Chesed.

The Tetragrammaton

If we look at the potency of the Divine Name of Chokmah, the Hebrew Letters of the Paths connecting Tiphareth, Chesed and Chokmah that form YHVH, the Tetragrammaton or Sacred Name of GOD.

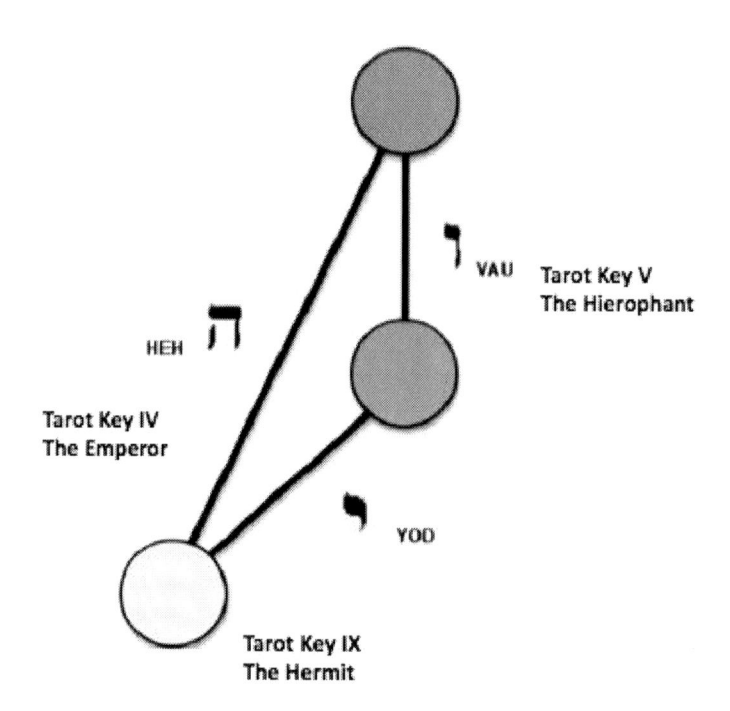

Fig. 37

For each of the Paths a Tarot card is assigned. If we follow the sequence of YHVH, we begin with The Hermit (inner reflection), move to The Emperor (a place of authority and glory), move to the

Hierophant (teacher of Higher Knowledge and guidance) and finally, move back to the Emperor. So, another way of looking at the energy of Chokmah would be to think in terms of the results of turning and moving within to seek Higher spiritual direction and teaching which moves us to a place of claiming more of our Divinity or Glory. Feeling imbued and empowered by our Divine nature we become the teacher and we seek those teachers and guides for us who will enrich and enliven this experience of ourselves as Divine Beings. Having received what is needed in any given time we return once again to our place of Glory; this time in a different state of mind and spirit. The seed like beginnings towards wisdom and greater understanding having been quickened.

The Spiritual Experience
The Vision of God Face to Face

The spiritual experience of Chokmah is that of the Vision of God face to Face. This experience is none that can be taken in human form, for to do so would be to cease to exist in that form. But, if we think of the energies of Chokmah we can easily imagine that this would be a natural byproduct having been the first form to emanate from that which is formless. This idea encompasses also the cyclic nature of this interaction. Kether having become aware of its formlessness and desiring to create more than Itself, does so in its own image. This awareness causes a reaction of response from that which is being observed (Chokmah). And, Chokmah can do nothing other than give response of awareness and recognition back to that which created it. In this way there is a dynamic that is set up, that if applied to the human experience can be likened to awareness and recognition of our Higher nature. It is our own creation and we its; so when we open to awareness and acknowledgement of it as part of our being we set into motion the reciprocity of exchange that allows us to ascend.

The Illusion of the Sphere
Independence

The illusion of Chokmah is that of Independence that is no longer in communication with the Higher nature. In essence it is divorcing oneself from the sacred union that is your birthright. In this way, the independent state is more divisive, rather than individualized which offers the polarity of natures with the understanding that each of the two are still contained within and part of the greater whole.

The Briatic Color
Grey

The Briatic color of Chokmah is grey. This coloring contains the white of Kether coming to a place of force and moving to a place of density by the time it reaches the blackness of Binah. Chokmah is the intermediary point standing between pure brilliance and density of light and flow contained within greater form.

Magickal Image
"A Bearded Male Figure"

The magickal image of Chokmah speaks to the energy of the Sage and the action that is required of him to ensure that creation will prevail. The image of having a beard denotes a certain maturity, that gives the impression of one who has come into an age of wisdom though the lessons learned from misdeeds and recklessness that often accompanies youth, as well as the responsibilities and creative outpour of life giving seed in the role as Father. If we take this attribution beyond its visual contrivances, we see that it is essentially the flow of the masculine nature. The force that is the precursor to form taking hold and redefining. And, just as the Sage gathers his lessons into himself and transforms them to a place of knowing and wisdom, so does the raw energy of this polarity draw from the infinite place of gnosis before issuing forth its wisdom.

Expression Through The Four Worlds

Atziluth - The Creative Urge
The Supreme Lord of Life

Atum - Odin - The Dagda

In the sphere of Chokmah, Atziluth is exemplified in the archetypal energy of those Deities from whose seed life is created. This life takes many forms and it is through the power of the supreme force of the "WORD" upon the waters of the formless energetic pattern that all is gathered to a point of useable and extricable form.

In its highest sense the Atziluth of Chokmah is the Great Name of Power that is the prime essence of the Divine Creator in its most refined and pure formless state. This name is considered the "name of names" or the Tetragrammaton, YHWH:

It is the completed form of the sacred name before it is separated (the Vau attributed to Binah and the Yod remains with Chokmah) and restructured into a place of form. It is the vibration of this name that calls worlds into being and ignites the catalytic spark towards the order of the Universe and all that is contained therein.

We see this in the archetype of Atum calling forth creation from his own seed and the waters of Nun. Odin was a god of battle, and also of wisdom, magick and poetry. His name means "fury" or "frenzy,", and in this potency of name is held a quality of fierce inspiration or dynamic force exerted to guide warriors and poets alike towards manifest creative outcome. Similarly, the Dagda of Celtic origins is known as the Father of the Celts, leader of the Tuatha de Danaan and god of knowledge. He is both destroyer and resurrector of the life force that is given.

Briah - Creation of a Concept - Archangel
Archangel Ratziel
"Guider of Creative Force"

The Archangel Ratziel is called the "one sent forth from God". His is the energy that disseminates the wisdom of cosmos and the universal truths held therein. His action is that of stirring the minds of men to see and reach beyond what is within their scope of understanding and to tap into the collective consciousness that is of the stars and the greater Universe. When these fires of understanding have been ignited and the desire to connect more fully in a broader scope arises we are heeding the call of Ratziel to take our place as co-creators of our cosmic experience.

Yetzirah - Forming the Image of the Concept
Angels - Auphanim
" The Wheels or The Encircling Ones"

The Auphanim are the organizers and directors of the force that emanates from Kether through Chokmah as it flows towards its mate in Binah. We discussed the process of the straight line emerging from the point and if we take this concept to the next level of action we can think of it in this way. The point of energy that is the brilliant urge of Kether moves towards Chokmah, extending itself in outreach and becoming the straight line of emanation. At the level of Chokmah, the Auphanim, in their potency as conductors, pull that straight line of energetic outpour into their cyclic core creating a spiral action of pattern and shape to be released in a cyclic type of action towards the goal of Binah. Think of being caught up in the spiraling force of a tornado, reaching the central point of calm and then the disbursement outward as contact is made with the outer edges of movement and motion.

Assiah - The World of Expression - Planetary
The Infinite Form of the Zodiac
Planet
The Zodiac

The Zodiac carries within its energies and attributes the cycle of evolutionary process at the level of the Cosmos. It holds the key to the cycles of life and death, manifest form to the formless and the lesson of the ultimate return to its state of beginnings and renewal. Each of the Twelve signs reflects an aspect that is vital to the process of the whole. At a human level the Zodiac offers the keys and blueprint that make each of us the individuals that we are and the precursor to the unique gifts and states of potential we have available in this lifetime. The wisdom of the Zodiac is held at a cellular and atomic level. Each of these signs taken independently show a piece of the picture, but taken together as a whole they unlock the keys to the Universe

The placement of the Zodiac within the sphere of Chokmah is the lesson of the all-encompassing cyclical nature of evolutionary process that is inherent within the structure of the zodiac itself. Each of the signs has its own energetic signature that is inclusive of modality and element. In this way all of the wisdom of the Universe and the greater plans of the Universe are accounted for and claimed within the process of attaining union with the Divine. This attribution also sets up the connection of space and limitlessness that works in contrast and in synchronicity with that of Binah and infinite Time. Time and Space being those components that form or disregard the boundaries and laws to which we imagine ourselves bound. It is the power that is exerted on time and space that if used wisely and correctly ensures the progression and expansion of the life force. It is this same power, if applied and used in wise manner it opens the potential within the individual to make best use of the inherent qualities available at the given time of birth.

The Living Tree: Personal Study

Opening to The Cosmic Rhythm

This set of exercises is intended to make you more aware of the greater world in which we live and attune you to the cosmic nature of our being.

Active Engagement (Part 1)

This exercise begins a study of your astrological blueprint. You want to find out what your Sun, Moon and Ascendant (or Rising) signs are. To gather this information you will need to know your:

- Date of Birth
- Geographic Location of Birth
- Time of Birth

An easy to navigate sight that will generate a free birth chart is **myastro.com**.

Journaling (Part 2)

1. In your journal using one full page for each. Write down your sun sign, your moon sign and the astrological sign of your Ascendant (or rising) signs.
2. Beginning with your sun sign, do some research into what the energies and attributes of that astrological sign are. Look through several books or sites on the internet, so you can gather as much information as possible.
3. When you have gathered what you feel is enough information, set aside some time to sit in quiet meditative

reflection. Look through what you have written down. Close your journal and then allow yourself to be open to receiving the pieces of that information that you feel most closely resonate to yourself. This is the place of moving from simply taking in and adding more pieces of knowledge and actively experiencing the information, forming conclusions and then drawing from the wisdom or essence of what you have learned.

4. Do this for your moon and ascendant signs. Keeping records in your journal use this information as the beginnings of gaining more insight about yourself. It is not without reason that "Know Yourself" was carved at the entrance to the Temple of the Oracle of Delphi. Your astrological blue print is unique to you and contains everything you need to know to be effective, productive and enlivened being.

Chapter Ten

KETHER

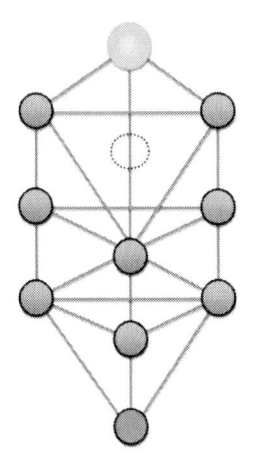

CROWN

Nothing and everything
The endless void fills all time
Until...

One moves in the silence
Stretching and reaching
Towards the other as two
Swiftly take flight.

They mingle and join
Each claiming their own side
So three may point the way.
Each base stretched far and wide.

Foundations are laid
By another close at hand
Who opens the four sealed gates.
Disruption and creative force

Issues forth as the skillfully crafted
Shield of focus reflects the five.

The light is fixed
The seeker is found
As outpour of healing grace
Gives way to the
Harmonious six.

Each walks a path of experience
Pulling and gathering from
Vista's extremes.
Wisdom and lessons hard won
Fill what moves within.

As six expands to become seven
The meandering web that
Connects becomes entwined.

A continuum of dual
Portal opening and eight
The final climax of force contained.

Like amoebas they move and
Wiggle and stretch and pull
And strain until the
Tension and release
Catapult them over
The initiatory threshold of
Death's nine gates.

All scatter and disperse
Once again seamlessly
Part of the void of the all
Until…

Once again the singular one rises
Reaching out towards its
Newly quickened mate.

Keywords

Pure Spirit/Consciousness

Master Prototype
Movement from a state of un-manifest nothing to a place that has the potential of becoming something

Attainment
Union with the Source of All Being

Completion
Ascension or Go Back to Home (Malkuth)

The Lesson of the Sphere

We have now reached the Source or the singular prime point of creation in its descent towards manifest form. We spoke in earlier chapters of an analogy of the flood-lights in a theater. The lights themselves are pure white, but with the addition of colored gels that cover the lights something new is created. Specific moods and nuances are evoked. Each light appears to be different, yet if you strip it back to its core state, they are all singular white lights.

As we have moved through our lessons we have noted how the different colorings and densities of energy have transformed, transmuted and become the varied and differing states of consciousness as assigned to each of the spheres; yet they are still part of and are inclusive of the singular point of downpour which emanates from Kether. The final goal of the Qabalist is to attain the consciousness of the Nothing.

With that last statement being made, one would think that this would be the longest chapter of all. But, in fact, reaching for words to explain and describe that which is not easily or ably articulated is just a futile attempt. The information is at once overwhelming and enlightening, complex and simple in its understanding. These are the energies that are experienced rather than spoken. These are the rare and brief mind touches that occur as we open and connect to our Divine nature. It is towards Kether that we aspire and it is in Malkuth that we complete our Great Work.

The Energy of the Sphere
What's in a Name?

Kether is assigned a variety of names and attributions. To some degree these are influenced by the essence of its energy as much as the cultural and occult clues to the nature of the sphere that are contained within. Below is a listing of some of the more widely used names:

- Existence of Existence
- The Concealed of the Concealed
- The Ancient of the Ancient Ones

As you see from the semantics of the three above, the duality or doubling causes a unique polarity to arise. It is also a greater emphasis that is given to the attribute described, which alludes to the timelessness of the energetic construct of Kether. This is the construct of both the **Primordial Point** and the **Point within the Circle.**

These last two attributions concern the natural symmetry and geometry contained within creation. The primordial point is that place where all was, is and shall be. It is the beginning and the end of what may unfold within its cycles. The Point within the circle is the extension outwards of that energetic creation. It is a pushing outwards and still containing the cyclical nature that is repeated throughout the cosmos. It holds both that which has been created and is also the Source of that creation itself. Kether is the point of all beginnings and the point towards which in the final inspiration of breath all that is manifest returns.

What Lives in the Great Above

The Three Veils of Negative Existence

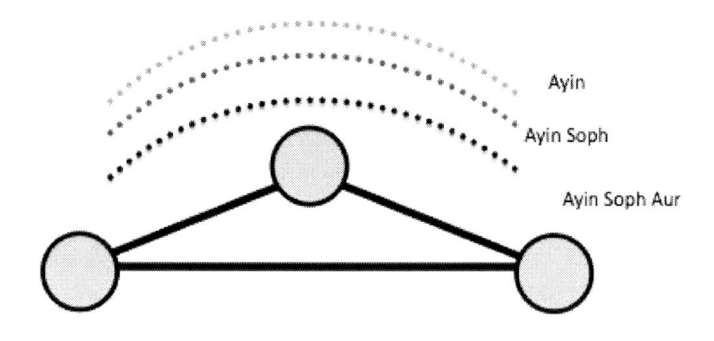

Fig. 38

The veils reside above the tree and represent the levels of non-existence just prior to creative force. This is the space of the Great Unmanifest Universe.

Ayin is translated as "nothing" and is the highest and furthest away from Kether. It is the complete absence of existence.

Ayin Soph is the middle veil that emanates in turn from Ayin and is the space of no limit. It is force that is formless and without container or restraint of limitation.

Ayin Soph Aur is the closest veil to the Tree itself and emanates from the limitless nature of Ayin Soph. It means "limitless or eternal light".

In consideration of the sphere of Kether, it is these Three Veils that create the stimulation, urge and subsequent action towards the Great emanation that is the downpour of Kether, the Crown itself reaching towards matter.

The Divine Spark

The sphere of Kether is the Divine Spark that initiates the stages of creation. If we consider the Supernals, Chokmah is the creative vessel, which holds the Divine Spark in preparation for its eventual initiatory experience of birth within the waters of Binah.

Within the energy of Kether we find the Urge and Yearning for more than Itself. IT serves as the master prototype for all that follows. This Divine desire creates the needed flow of energy to satisfy that yearning, and directs its course through that of Chokmah and then towards Binah.

Kether is called the Crown. I like to think of this in the sense that a ruler's crown is that which sits apart and is separate, yet still very much a part of the human or physical being who wears it. It is the "idea" that is evoked when in the company of one who wears the "Crown" and the potency of that expression contained within the "understood" authority and power now considered part of that person's dominion.

The virtue of Kether is that of attainment. The continuous cycle and flow of energy, birth, death, evolution and involution are required to maintain the creative directive. Within the workings of the Universe all of life is in a constant state of creation. Having aspired upwards towards the source that created the realization is that of return to a state of potential; a state of formlessness which then can be returned into a place of form.

The Mystical Consciousness

The energy of Kether is one of Pure Consciousness that is unrestricted and flowing freely from the Creator, Itself. If we look at the definitions of the word Mystical, we gain a sense of the quality of a consciousness that is paradoxical in nature. **By definition Mystical is:**

1. Of or having a spiritual reality or import not apparent to the intelligence or senses.

2. Of, relating to, or stemming from direct communion with ultimate reality or God

3. Enigmatic; obscure:

4. Unintelligible; cryptic.

To some degree consciousness implies awareness. This is, after all, the desired or "illumined" state that spiritual seekers pursue. The quality of obscurity to the intelligible senses gives clue that the nature of this conscious state is one that cannot be defined and connected to through purely logical and mental process. Emotion is the key that unlocks and reveals the mystery that is hidden within the consciousness of Kether. Compassion and yearning for unity with the Divine works upon the mental process, tearing down the limits that are imposed and thus revealing the true nature of the creative process.

The Hidden Intelligence

The wisdom and intelligence found in the sphere of Kether requires that it be sought out, and then, and only then, will the smallest glimpse of its true nature be revealed.

The paradigm is that it is only hidden because we choose not to see its glory. Albeit, these concepts are all philosophical in basis given that only that which is un-manifest can merge with and comprehend that which is also un-manifest, but the strivings towards the metaphors and applications of these energies is still relevant and concrete in the workings towards spiritual evolvement. In this way, that which is hidden is often in plain sight, if you have the "eyes" to perceive it.

The Element of the Sphere

Root of Air (Air of Air)

Kether is assigned the element of **Root of Air**. It was upon the breath of the first word that the world and all of life was created. It is by the breath that all could similarly be destroyed. The pure essence of Air enfolded within itself is that of movement towards specialized and active goal. Air is the only element that cannot be seen other than by the products of its effects. We note the current of air as it moves across the surface of the waters. We note the fueling of air as the flames reach higher or are extinguished completely. We note the intensity of air by the gentle or frantic movement of the trees. We note the support of air as eagle wings stretch and life ascends. We trust that air is moving through our lungs and sustaining our bodies in support of maintaining life. We move through it in its varied forms of energy, sound and vibration.

So, too Kether is recognizable by its efforts, yet remains intangible, and undifferentiated in its presence. If we equate air with mind and intellect, the quality of Air of Air is mind that moves with the deftness and a gentle spring's breeze and the intensity of a blustery wind storm. It is ever present and non-existent at will and moves at a speed that is neither of time nor space because it is both Time and Space.

Numerical Value

Kether stands as the **First** Sphere on the Tree of Life. Within the energy of the number **1** is not only the place of singularity, but also a foundation from which the potential to replicate and create in its own diffuse image is contained. It is the beginning and also the point of completion and there is choice to be made regarding that status. It may stay inert and alone or may choose to seek out, diversify and through the ending of its singular nature move towards polarity and duality.

In looking at the shape and form of the number l, it is not difficult to visualize the concept of a singular point reaching downwards towards extension as the other point of origin reaches upwards towards expansion. Each point of origin blending seamlessly into a single line of continuous movement of return and release that holds within its structure the potential for movement in any direction and creation of something new. In the sphere of Kether it is exactly this nature that creates the continuum of ITSELF, expressed through the division of ITSELF.

Location on the Tree

The Pinnacle Sphere on the Pillar of Equilibrium

The Middle Pillar is the equalizer or place of balance where the Greater Work is synthesized. This is the place of the rising Kundalini, the lunar and solar pathways combined and the greater knowledge of Life, Death and Rebirth. This is the Pillar of Consciousness in its ascent (The Serpent of Wisdom) the catalyst for evolution. And, the Pillar of Grace in its descent from Kether to Malkuth becomes the path of involution. The Spheres of this pillar are Malkuth, Yesod, Tiphareth and Kether.

THE CROWN

BEAUTY

FOUNDATION

KINGDOM

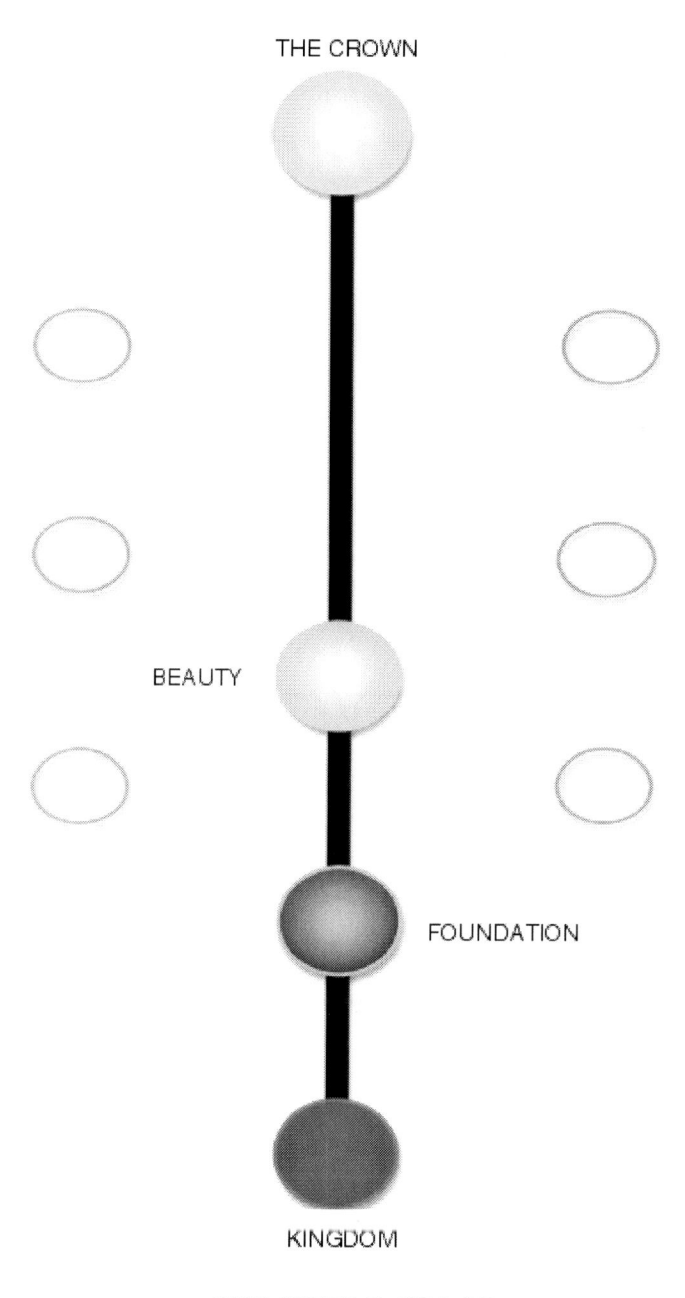

THE MIDDLE PILLAR

Fig. 39

The Spiritual Experience
The Vision of Unity

The spiritual experience of Kether is that of the Vision of Unity. This is the Vision of Return, and in that return the individualization of the whole is unified once again. In this rarified state the formless nature of its energy, the thought or idea of separateness is no longer valid. This is the state of the final initiation of death, when manifest form is released and Spirit moves again towards it original pattern that is one and the same as the cosmos from which it came.

The Briatic Color
White Brilliance

In the supernal spheres we see colors of value, light and dark. The black of Binah holds all the colors within its darkness. Chokmah is the lighter value of the darkness of Binah. It too, still contains a spectrum of all the colors, but the essence has been diluted by the brilliance of Kether. Kether is pure Light, but within this brilliance of Light is held the potential for other spectrums of color depending on the refraction and qualities of the filters through which it processes. Think in terms of a beautiful, crystalline prism and what occurs when pure brilliant Light is refracted through it.

The Magickal Image
"An Ancient Bearded King Seen in Profile "

The magickal image of Kether is that of an Ancient Bearded King Seen in Profile. This image immediately evokes several trains of thought. The figure is that of a King, a title that denotes a state of authority and command. The fact that this King is Ancient and Bearded adds the dynamics of time; or more aptly the passing a large amount of time. This is authority that has been tempered by experience. There is a state of maturity; rather than the fool-hearty and impetuous nature of youth. This figure is seen in profile.

Another key to the mystery of Kether. For, none may see the full face of the creator in all its glory and remain incarnate in existence. There is, again, much relevance in a poem by the poet, Rumi called "His Glory". It describes aptly the incomprehensible nature of that which cannot be articulated. This experience being intensely personal and transcendent in nature such that those who are still tied to incarnate form have only the briefest glimpse of pure refined state of discarnate Beingness.

Expression Through The Four Worlds

We have, in reaching Kether, also reached the apex of the elements as examined within the Four Worlds. The world of Atziluth is that of Fire acting upon the world of Briah; moving through its waters that are both carrier and container. Yetzirah breathes the Word of Life into those fluid states of movement and from their depths manifestation comes into being in the World of Assiah. As we have stated previously, all four of the worlds are carried within each of the spheres, acting upon their specific energies with every sphere below Kether reaching further downward into a state of dense and formed matter.

Within the prime sphere of Kether, these worlds ebb and flow, each into the other shifting and changing tides between outward pulse and in-spired breath. Each in its most refined and essential state. Each existing as the godhead of creation within its own realm.

Atziluth - The Creative Urge

The Supreme Lord of Life
The Great "I Am"

In the sphere of Kether, the principle of the Supreme Lord of Life is taken in its most literal sense. It is both formless and timeless and its energy is that of being the "cause" of manifest form. It is the Source from which all else came into being. In this sense we may place those Gods who are considered the Fathers or Rulers of all of the Gods. In this form we also see that Kether is not only the energy from which issues forth others, but that there is mastery and authority over that process and that what is brought into existence is so wholly a part of itself that it also is Divine in nature.

Briah - Creation of a Concept - Archangel
Archangel Metatron
"The Angel of the Presence"

The Archangel Metatron is seen as Sandalphon in the world of Malkuth. His name is derived from the Greek "meta ton tronos" meaning "near thy throne". His is the energy that filters and moves the primal energy of the Creator towards its goal of manifestation. Metraton communes with the supreme Creator and instills in man the feeling of Divinity that stirs his aspiration upwards towards an evolved state of consciousness.

Yetzirah - Forming the Image of the Concept
Angels
" The Four Holy Creatures "

The entities that are attributed to the sphere of Kether are the Four Holy Creatures. The Four Holy Creatures are the Higher experience of the Kerubim of Malkuth. In their evolved states they encompass the necessary foundations and components to produce Form from that which is Form-less. These are represented as the Winged Man, the Eagle, the Winged Lion and the Winged Bull. We also see that these are the Fixed signs of the Zodiac: Taurus - Leo - Scorpio - Aquarius

The Four Holy Creatures

Ox/Bull	Lion	Eagle	Man
♉	♌	♏	♒
Strength	Courage	Swiftness	Intelligence
Patience	Nobility	Aspiration	Devotion

These Fixed signs represent sustainability, longevity and permanence and form the central points or core of foundation. It is from this foundation that the energy of Kether flows in a cardinal (building, burgeoning) method of creation and once that creation is stabilized, the energy is sent out in a mutable (flexible, resilient) way of release towards its manifest form.

A further lesson of the action of the Four Holy Creatures lies in the law that in order to act as creator, we hold mastery over the elements that permeate the world(s) in which we are creating. These elements are that of:

- Air/breath or the speaking of the WORD.
- Fire/Will and Desire to reach beyond the confines of Itself.
- Water/the condenser through which creative energy may be conducted.
- Earth/the container and the result of the creative effort.
- And, in the case of Kether, the Fifth element, that of Spirit.

It is the synthesized, pure essence of Kether that transmutes those elements into useable and creative form. It is fitting that these Four Holy Creatures also represent the Ages of Humanity. For Humanity as a collective whole itself must transit through the elements of evolution before coming full cycle back to the primordial place of its collective creation.

Assiah - The World of Expression - Planetary

The First Swirlings

Kether is the Primum Mobile, an original creator, from the Latin meaning "first cause or first mover". These first swirlings are composed of Nebulae. Diffuse nebulae are clouds of interstellar matter, namely thin but widespread agglomerations of gas and dust. These are the swirlings of cosmic dust, which through its pure and directed Force gave rise to Form.

The Living Tree: Personal Study

Opening to The Limitless ALL

This set of exercises is intended to make you more aware of the tendency to pause in focus on those things that are not of real importance, and rush through those that should be given the necessary attention and then offered up to the natural flow of outcome.

Meditative Focus

Practice the art of Mindfulness Meditation. Sit comfortably in a quiet setting and allow whatever thoughts wish to present to flow easily through your mind. Consciously acknowledge each one and then let it pass freely. Make note of any thoughts that are persistent and/or continue to present themselves. These may be areas for further exploration. And often these will blossom into those things that are waiting for you to bring into manifestation

Chapter Eleven

DA'AT

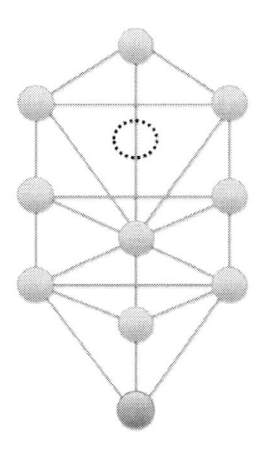

KNOWLEDGE

The Hidden Path

What sound issues forth
From the place of the
Abyss.

It is neither the timbre
Of sweet angelic choir
Nor the shrieks and
Howls of those
Souls lost in the night.

It is not the harmonious
Cadence of the Universe
Or the persistent hum
Of time moving from
Point to point.

Perhaps, it is the silent
Pause between the beats
Of a heart that has given
All that it has to give.

This is the silence that
Is full of potential and
Hover just at the edge
Of ecstasy bursting forth.

It is the hollow echo
That stirs the memory
And opens the sight
To choices and paths
Taken long ago.

It is the primal scream
That heralds the beginning
Or renewed awareness.

It is the silent scream
Of the Fool as he steps
Off the edge of what is known
And falls into the arms of
True Knowledge.

The Hidden Sphere

> " Whatever affects one directly, affects all indirectly.
> I can never be what I ought to be until you
> are what you ought to be. This is the interrelated
> structure of reality."
> - Dr. Martin Luther King, Jr. -

Until recent times, Da'at was not included in the listing of the Sephiroth. Its energies were considered to be more that of a state of being versus an emanation in the strictest sense of the word. This

Awareness is exemplified in the movement towards the sphere of Binah. Her planetary energy is that of Saturn, Gatekeeper of Time, organization and structured action.

Binah's Other Names

The Invisible Sephirah, The Hidden or Unrevealed Cosmic Mind, The Mystical Sephirah, The Upper Room, Sphere of the Greater Masters Gnosis

The Lesson of the Sphere

The sphere of Chesed held the energy of mastery over all things. Stepping across the threshold and onto the hidden path of Da'at we move towards the unified energies of the Archangels of the Four Cardinal Directions Uriel (North) - Raphael (East) - Michael (Fire) and Gabriel (Water). Mastery of these forces has now integrated into deep gnosis or ALL-knowingness of their inner workings- without the interface of boundary. This is the hidden knowledge or mystery that is held within each of the Mighty Ones and when brought to a place of union establishes the final individualization of the personality.

Its order of angels are those of the Winged Serpents. These beings hold the knowledge of both good and evil, dark and light, and rise as the Kundalini to their point of union and enlightenment. They are not the fiery serpents of Geburah, but rather those of a highly refined luminescence that holds the divine spark within and can only be seen by those who have attained a clarity of sight.

Location on the Tree

The Point of Union

Da'at represents the stage of spiritual evolution where the Soul has achieved its highest purpose and no longer has need to be at the mercy of ego and lower mental process. It is the juncture of union with the energy of the spheres of the Supernal Triangle. This is the consummate joining of force and form to produce the progeny of Chokmah and Binah's coalesced natures and bring it forth in clarity of mind through Da'at's expression. Da'at sits in the place of gnosis, knowledge having been refined and absorbed into the consciousness of being. This communion is one in which the Divine Spark is the point of contact as divine life returns to ITs source.

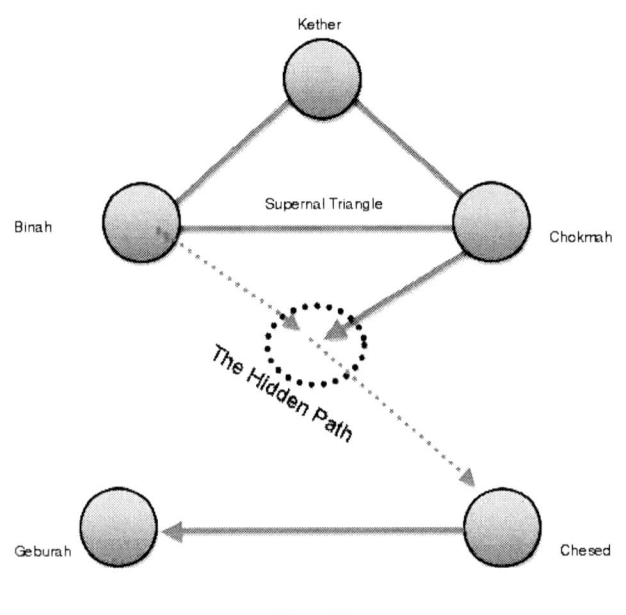

Fig. 40

The Energetic Component

Each of the creative fires have in turn been fueled by the Air of Tiphareth (strategically just below Da'at). These have blazed the way for transformation of the lower mental, the emotional and is now concerned with transmutation of the Higher Mind, which can only be realized in releasing the ego of personality and crossing the Abyss.

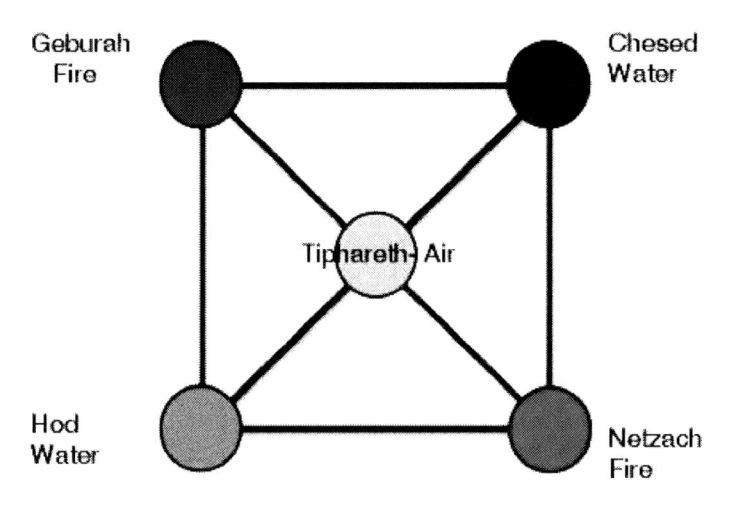

```
         Geburah                        Chesed
          Fire          ●──────────●     Water
                         \  \    /  /
                          \   \ /   /
                           \   ╳   /
                            \ / \ /
                         Tiphareth  Air
                            / \ / \
                           /   ╳   \
                          /   / \   \
                         /  /     \  \
          Hod           ●──────────●   Netzach
         Water                          Fire
```

The Energetic Triad
Fire - Water - Air

Fig. 41

The Gateway of Da'at

This bears repeating from Chapter Seven, the sphere of Chesed, to see the complete relationship and totality of the combined efforts of will and surrender.

Chesed is the last sphere on ascending the Tree before stepping into the realm of the Supernals of Kether, Chokmah and Binah. It is the place of final choice that has been informed by the energy of the spheres below it and the decision to .brave crossing the abyss to reach the womb of the Great Mother (Binah). It is the Gateway to both Wisdom (Chokmah) and Understanding (Binah).

By choosing this path and crossing the Abyss, you have relinquished control and placed yourself at the Mercy of what trials and challenges lay in wait for you. The courage that is called up is bolstered by the experience of moving from the sphere of Chesed; where unconditional love was offered up. The hope that is held forward is in the understanding that if successful in this journey, the waters of life (Binah) will draw you back towards your place of origin.

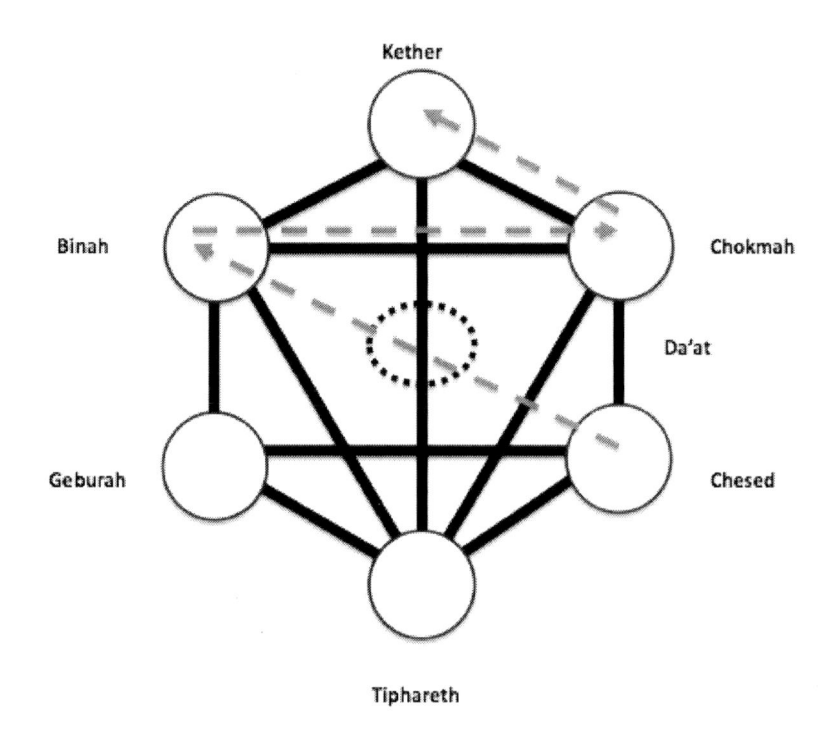

Fig. 42

The Spiritual Experience

Vision of Crossing the Abyss

The vision that Da'at provides is that of seeing clearly and with non-attachment the way of profound balance. Having claimed those shadow aspects and seen through the veil of illusion of duality to the core of its true nature as combined and cohesive force the strivings of the now individualized personality flow into the consciousness of oneness. It is at this point that memory and dynamics of past, present and future merge to become a singular point of existence as the great bridge is crossed and the arms of the Great Mother extend outward in receipt.

The Illusions and Virtues of the Sphere

Virtues and Vices

Virtue- Detachment, Perfection of Justice, Confidence in the future

Vice- Doubt of the future, Apathy, Inertia, Pride, Cowardice

Justice- Drawing on the guidance of the Higher Self that is devoid of EGO and guided by the merciful seeing of the larger whole. This allows that which must fall to the wayside do so with the strength of knowing it is for the greater good.

This form of justice is inconceivable to Man. It encompasses and encapsulates the whole of the cosmic and universal laws, order and realms, inclusive of all the beings residing therein. This justice is expressed in the development of the Soul.

The Magickal Image

"A Head with Two Faces Looking Both Ways "

The magickal image of Da'at reflects the necessary attention to what has been left behind and what we are reaching towards. It is this state of awareness that is needed to successfully cross the Abyss. We yearn to leave some part of ourselves in the past, yet are compelled to step out into the unknown of the future, being mindful of the goings on in both venues and keeping a watchful eye(s) so that all will proceed as planned. In this way, we are present in both states of existence and are able to use the experience of both to inform our next steps.

Crossing The Abyss

*As far as we can discern,
the sole purpose of human existence
is to kindle a light
in the darkness of mere being.*

.. Carl G. Jung ..

The goal of a seeker on the path is to come to a place of balance between chaos and order, good and evil, the dark and light that we hold within. Resistance and fear of the results can halt progress in its tracks and following the needs and desires of ego and personality wanting to remain in control do little to elevate our consciousness. To stand at the Threshold of the Abyss is to bring awareness to the darker nature and shadow aspects. Until these aspects are brought under the domain and power of the void of Da'at contact and connection with the Supernals is never achieved. It is at that juncture that we have come upon the divergent path that offers choice of either embrace or retreat. So, what exactly is this shadow self?

The Dark Night of The Soul

The concept of the Dark Night of the Soul is one that is experienced at specific points on the Tree and of varying intensities. It is described as a state of utter loneliness, despair and the sense that the Divine has forsaken you. It is a moment that stands the test of true "faith" for in that hour of disconnect the realization of separateness and the intense yearning for union with the Divine are brought to the forefront of the experience. This descent into a type of abyss is what serves to strengthen the resolve and conviction of the human and releases the vestiges of ego and personality that do not serve well the spiritual nature.

A Lesser form of this test of faith and spiritual strength comes upon the 27th Path, connecting Hod and Netzach. The Tarot Key of The Tower is placed upon this path and it is the work of the combined energies of Hod (Mind) and Netzach (Heart) to shatter the faulty foundations of our "ivory towers". The intensity of energetic response that occurs when pure mind and informed heart struggle to collaborate and become co-creators in creating a more enlightened state of being tests the seekers entire system of beliefs and understandings. Overwhelming darkness, depression, doubt and inertia are the natural byproducts until surrender to the process reveals the greater light of Tiphareth above.

Embracing the Shadow Self

To continue this stream of thought and in keeping with the refinement of energies and forces as we ascend the Tree we see these dynamics held within the "hidden path" of Da'at. It is on this path that a Dark Night of the Soul is replicated at a Higher Level of refinement and offers up test once again of the faith and Knowledge (Da'at) that has been worked upon as result of emanation from Tiphareth to Geburah, and finally arriving at Chesed. This is the call to final surrender of personality and ego to enter the Supernals of Higher Mind and the Triad of Creation (Kether, Chokmah and Binah). It is at this juncture that the shadow or darker nature of the self is met and aligned with its polarity of Light.

This surrender to the dark nature held within is a means of opening to the greater Light. And, this great light is ultimately the way of illumination on ascent through the spheres of the Middle Pillar that culminates in union with the brilliance of Kether. The pain of this endurance is at once physical, spiritual and mental and it is at the point of the darkest hour when the darkness seems most pervasive that the ultimate reflection of Kether's brilliance points the way.

Facing the Shadow

At some point along a spiritual path we must also encounter what is often called the "shadow self". This is an important milestone towards forward movement, and it is at that juncture that we have come upon the divergent path that offers choice of either embrace or retreat. So, what exactly is this shadow self?

According to Carl Jung, there are within the human experience and consciousness several highly specialized archetypes that define the human psychological experience. These archetypes are closely linked to our physical nature and are often brought to the surface through the varied preconditioned responses that we have gathered from our environment of both instinctual and mental learning. These become the patterns that play out in our lives in a continuous thread until some upheaval of either a conscious or unconscious level brings out what has lain hidden within our psyche.

This often plays out in the form of projection; or seeing the negative traits in others we encounter that are actually in resonance to those same qualities within ourselves, albeit latent and for the most part unacknowledged at a conscious level.

Down the Rabbit Hole

Beginning shadow work can be a bit like going down the rabbit hole. It is not the most comfortable process and what may be lurking at the base of that unknown can be daunting.

Many times what you thought to be true for yourself will be challenged and tested as you reveal some of the underlying reasons for the way in which you move through life. We all wish to be seen in a positive light and the work of exploring our shadow self can provide clues and greater understanding of those qualities we wish to enhance and accentuate, those that we hold in reserve for the appropriate times and those that serve no useful purpose in this lifetime other than now we are more aware of those characteristics in a way that is informed. Additionally, this is a journey that only you can make with only your own resources, experiences and inner knowing as guides.

The Mirror of SELF

*To confront a person with his own shadow
is to show him his own light.*

.. Carl G. Jung ..

As the quote above beautifully states, embracing those parts of yourself that are not usually brought into the light of day can, nonetheless, open the doorway to the greater light that ever burns within our being. If we think in terms of polarity and synthesis than we must acknowledge that the darkness only appears dark because we know of the polarity of light. Each gives validation, support and energy to the other in an, albeit transparent, way. Each relying on the other's existence to support and enhance the other's. This becomes the point of synthesis and understanding that within this process of give and take, each must contain a portion of the other within itself as the move through their dance of cohesion and balance.

The Midnight Sun

If we hold these principles as viable occurrences within a natural order of being, then we could also say that in the darkest night the sun is still brilliantly shining whether we can see it from the perspective we are aligned with. But, with a shift of geographical coordinates, we move into its light and what was night becomes day.

This concept is useful when approaching our darker nature. Despite what we may find lurking in the darkened corners of our personality, there is still shining that inner light that connects us with our higher state of being. When we learn to accept, acknowledge and embrace those parts of ourselves that we consider unlovable or undesirable we open to having conversation with those aspects and strengthen the potential to modify, change or completely transform that energy.

The nature of the work and the feelings and sensations that are often brought to the surface are not easily dealt with on your own; regardless of your own personal level of experience. To set foot within the scope of these energies is arduous and often painful and could do damage to the psyche if not approached slowly, carefully and with the utmost of respect. It is best to do a little research first rather than diving right into this type of work as it can dredge up past memories and experiences that may cause unproductive discomfort. Be gentle with yourself and approach this work slowly and with reverence, affirming the best results for your highest good.

And, as with each spiritual endeavor, always be mindful that the greatest journey we take is that which is the path leading back to ourselves, in dark and in light that returns us to our Divine nature.

Part Three

Pathworkings Within the Tree

Pathworkings Within the Tree

How to Use These Pathworkings

There are many ways to imprint the information about each of the qabalistic spheres in your memory. One of the ways that is used in magickal study is through the use of a Pathworking.

Pathworkings differ from guided mediations in that, if skillfully constructed, each component, object, location or color is meant to open your subconscious to a deeper level of understanding. Each word and the way in which you arrive at, leave or interact with a space calls up a stored memory of experience in this or other lifetimes that reveals yet another key to the larger puzzle of our Soul's purpose.

Additionally, these pathworkings can be used to establish a regular meditation practice that will make your mind more receptive to all manner of information and studies.

Good- Read through the pathworking each time you want to use the pathworking. Make note of pausing in the reading wherever it feels like more time would be spent in the specific train of thought.

Better- Read through the pathworking several times and as you do so, try to set up key points that are stored in the memory. In this way, you can create your own scenarios using the structure of the original pathworking without having to read through the text each time.

Best- Employ the physicality (Malkuth) of recording the pathworking in your own voice which produces an effective recognizable neurological imprint inducing physiological response and imprint to listen to.

When you are ready to make the recording be sure to select a space where you will not be interrupted and has minimal background noise.

Be sure to speak slowly (more so, if you tend to speak quickly and do not annunciate well) and clearly and to give pause where it would naturally occur if you were reading aloud. There may be some points in the meditation where you will want to spend several minutes in the locale that is being presented. Remember to give adequate time of silence for this. Do not stop the recording, pause and restart it. Allow the amount of time you wish to have to fill the space on the recording and then resume the reading of the pathworking.

Regardless of what method you use, remain open and receptive to what presents to you beyond what has been scripted through the pathworking as you move more deeply into this study. Having a journal to record your impressions and keeping record of your progress in memorizing the information and making use of a journal can serve as great encouragement to you. Looking back and seeing how far you have come fuels the desire and gives you markers of growth that are concrete, tangible and acknowledgement of your hard work.

Note: If you wish to use these as meditative tools, begin with the pathworking for the sphere of Malkuth. Dedicate a full month to its use; deepening each session to open to the energies of the particular sphere. The following month proceed to the sphere of Yesod. Again, dedicate a full month to its use and integration. Spend some time at the end of each meditation session thinking on how the sphere of focus interacts with and relates to the previous and the next in the path of the Lightening Flash. You will be amazed at the insight gained and the groundwork laid towards fully incorporating the Tree into your daily practice.

The Sphere of Malkuth: Earth, My Home

Turn your focus and attention to your breath. Allow your consciousness to move with the rise and fall of your chest and the filling and release of the lungs. Continue in this manner for several breaths; allowing each to become softer, smoother and slower

You step out onto a well-worn path, the earth beneath your feet still moist from the mist of the morning and tall full green trees form a canopy through which strands of early morning light gently stretch and extend to light the way.

You can feel the electricity of life all around you- insect- animal- bird-leaf- tree and rich fertile earth. You sense a connection and the interconnectedness between yourself and your surroundings. Excited and anxious to explore more of this place, you move forward on the path. Each footfall announced by the gentle crackling of crisp leaf and twig underfoot. As you move along the Path it seems as though all of your senses become heightened and alive in a way that you have not felt for a long time.

Color, shape and form take on more depth and detail. You hear every sound that surrounds you, drawing you into an intimate conversation with the natural forces. You can smell each of the wild flowers, their individual aromas filling each nostril in a kaleidoscope of essence all mingling and the scent of damp rich earth gives a feeling of foundation as the scent of all animal life wafts gently on the breeze affirming that you are not alone.

You reach out, hand extended and fingers reaching to touch a cascading bough of leaves from a graceful willow tree and you can feel the pulse of energy rush through your being. A connection between earth and sky above circulates and weaves a spiral pattern through your very core. There is greenery all around you, and as you walk further along this path the beauty of this earth realm wells up inside and fills you with awe.

You now see just ahead of you a clearing of open field and brilliant sunlight. The noonday sun has arrived and feathery shoots of wheat fill this space. They are ochre in color with variations of tan and brown interspersed in accord with their readiness for harvest. As you walk into the center you feel the gentle brushes of plant life and the softness of earth beneath in support of this place of growth. You look upwards towards the sky and the warmth of the noonday sun floods across your face and you think upon the brilliance of the Divine shining and reflected back to you. You are in a sea of life, but this is also the place of sacrifice- the cutting of the wheat and harvest- as well as a place of return; for that wheat will also serve to nourish and feed. You think on these things and bask in the warmth of the sun before moving on.

As you turn towards the North you notice a small mound of earth, just at the edge of this clearing. Hard stone and rock create the sculptures of the Gods. At the very base of one of the smaller rocks you are surprised to find an exposed area of russet colored clay-like dirt. It is more brown than red, but you have a sense of the red moving through it as blood moves through veins. Enlivening and adding richness and fire to this patch of earth. You bend down and move your fingers over and through the clay, marveling at how moist it is. It smells different than the moist earth and you intuitively know that any plant life would draw its nutrients from what lay on the top of this soil. It is life reaching upwards for sustenance, while being supported by the strength of earth below.

You have been so intent on the diversity of all you have found that you become aware that the sun is beginning to set and you must return through the woods to your place of beginning. Once again you walk through the wheat-covered field and take note of the change in color as the shadows of the night move across the expanse of feather-like face. You hear the call of the wolf in the distance and see the first fluttering of bat wings moving above. As you step once again onto the path into the woods, there is a moment of darkness and blackness all around. But, in that state of darkness it is neither menacing nor a place of fear. Rather, there is great comfort in the swaddling of the night and the union of earth and sky cradling you. Clouds move in unison and the brilliant light of the moon is revealed, lighting the path; moonbeams replacing those of the early sun you previously experienced. All takes on new shape and form in this moonlit scene and yet remains the same, only its outer appearance changing in accord with the shadow or brilliance of light. You move in rhythm with the energy surrounding you and draw on the synthesis of experience you have had on and beyond this path. You know that there is much that lays hidden and longs to be revealed, but for now this is the beginning of a journey back to your true Nature.

As you stand once again at the place of your physical being, the swirling of time and space encircle you. You have walked the circle of the Earth and her elements. This is one of the keys the sphere of Malkuth holds in its mysteries. The gift of manifest form. This is the receiving place of the combined energy of all the spheres above, emanating downward into the Kingdom of the Four who find their strength in the return to the One.

The woods and all they contain gently fade from your sight and you begin the descent back into your physical state of being and the room and space in which you began this pathworking. Return to awareness of the rhythm of your breath and the rise and fall of your chest. Become aware of the physicality of where you are sitting or laying; your body pressed against cushion, chair or floor.

And when you are ready, gently flutter your eyes open

The Sphere of Yesod: Temple of the Moon

Turn your focus and attention to your breath. Allow your consciousness to move with the rise and fall of your chest and the filling and release of the lungs. Continue in this manner for several breaths; allowing each to become softer, smoother and slower.

You step out onto a well-worn path and you can smell the dampness of the earth and can make out the silhouettes of the trees surrounding you. Above, the sky is velvety black and the moon shines down like a spot light creating a circle of light around you. This is Malkuth; your physical world. Take a moment to look around. As you stand in this circle of moonlit space a violet mist swirls around you. It encircles and embraces you within its violet glow and you feel as though you are being lifted upwards.

You feel what appears to be soft ground beneath your feet and the swirling mist has now changed into ribbons of indigo colored cloth. The cloth is gauzy and light and is moving quite rapidly although there is no apparent breeze. You are unsure of the origins of this movement and as you begin to focus on this thought the swaths of indigo cloth appear to fade. As your eyes adjust to the dimness of light, you realize that what you thought were ribbons of cloth now are seen as beams of milky white light. You look down and see that what you thought was soft ground beneath is a cottony grey mist that does not seem dense enough to hold your weight. Things are not as they appear in this realm and you make mental note to give pause before making judgment of what you experience here.

As you become more accustomed to the surroundings your senses begin to heighten and you can feel an energy that seems full of many different particles of light, and although the form and shapes are not clear you intuit that there is great potential in what encloses you. You look down and see that what you are standing upon has no distinct shape and there appear to be rhythmic pulses within the misty grey depths of this landscape. Outlines of form move and rise to the surface. Some contract back into the grayness and others seem to rise upwards and fade out of sight, never taking solid form. You remember that in the space of Malkuth color, shape and form took on more depth and detail. You could hear every sound. Everything here seems to be just a fleeting image or the muffled sound of something you are unsure of. Everything is just out of grasp of clearly defining its limits and extensions.

As these and many more thoughts pass through your mind you become aware of the light changing as the moon emerges from a frothy cloud of deep purple. The moon is luminescent and you can almost feel the magnetic energy of its pull moving within you. You sense the resonance of the waters within your being and see them now as tides of time and change. The ebbing and flowing in accord with the natural cycles of the moon and the stars. You feel the interconnectedness of your being and the life that is contained within the quickening and potential of this space.

You sit down and wafts of soft grey mist respond to the movement. You close your eyes and soften your breath moving into a deep contemplative state. As you sit quietly memories flood through your mind. Pictures move like a slide show on your inner screen and all the wishes and dreams you have experienced in this lifetime bubble up to the surface. This is your storehouse of the subconscious. Some of the images are directly of your own creation and others have been colored and changed by the co-mingled energies of the collective consciousness. Some are useless daydreams and others hold the potential for new and inventive action.

As these images pass before you the urge to reach out and grasp one, to hold it and feel its weight and strength in your hands takes hold. The images begin to slow and one attracts your attention. You gently reach out and are surprised at the ease with which you were able to draw it to you. You make a mental note of how its energy feels in your hands and what emotions it may stir within you. You seem able to see more clearly what this image truly is and where the illusion of the situation may have been at the time of the first creation of this image. As you begin to give more attention and definition of clarity to this image you see that it is responding to this outpour. The color is now becoming a golden yellow. Within its core are flecks of azure, violet and deep purple. Each a spark of energy within a seed of growth containing a possibility and potential for manifestation. The energy forms more clearly into a sphere, the continuum of all that is contained within and the connection with all that is without. It glows and pulses within your hand with life. A flood outward of golden yellow and the sphere opens in spirals of the seeds of light that were within. Scattering like the seeds of the dandelion bulb as you blow on it and grey strands are caught within the winds embrace. You sit for a moment in the glow of this new birth and you feel transformed and changed. Moved to a place of greater understanding of how the Universe works and what is the driving and compelling force of the creative urge for life.

You stand and look once again upwards towards the moon. You now see with clearer intent and the mysteries of her nature will slowly reveal themselves as you continue to visit this realm of dreams and potential. But, for now you must return to the world of the physical. A mist of violet swirlings moves about you and you feel a gentle descent. Slowly and with great ease your feet touch down upon the damp soil of Malkuth.

As you stand once again at the place of your physical being, the swirling of time and space encircle you, the violet color giving way to the earthy colors of the physical realm. This is the receiving place of the combined energy of all the spheres above, emanating downward into the Kingdom of the Four who find their strength in the return to the One. You smell the earth upon which you make your home and feel the soft breeze of the winds. You see the silhouettes of the trees of the woods and hear the sounds of life all around you. Stand for a moment in this place.

The woods and all they contain gently fade from your sight and you begin the descent back into your physical state of being and the room and space in which you began this pathworking. Return to awareness of the rhythm of your breath and the rise and fall of your chest. Become aware of the physicality of where you are sitting or laying; your body pressed against cushion, chair or floor.

And when you are ready, gently flutter your eyes open

The Sphere of Hod: The Think Tank

Turn your focus and attention to your breath. Allow your consciousness to move with the rise and fall of your chest and the filling and release of the lungs. Continue in this manner for several breaths; allowing each to become softer, smoother and slower. With each breath your physical body appears to lighten and your center of consciousness floats upwards towards the inner eye. You feel enveloped by the mist of transition between the Physical and Astral.

As this veil thins and dissipates you see that you have arrived at the headquarters of the most prestigious Think Tank in the world. You are not sure why you have been asked here, but know that this is a great honor. As you move through the revolving door of this skyscraper you step into a beautiful marble lobby. Earthy colors of greens and blues decorate this space and as you walk forward you are greeted by a tall young man. He tells you he will be your guide and you are asked to follow him into an office. You step into the room and see that it is sparsely furnished and has a bit of damp earthy smell about it. The room has been decorated in earth tones and the chair upon which you are to sit is made of a beautiful dark wood. Momentarily distracted by your surroundings, you are called back to attention by the voice of your guide and told that you have been called to this place to think through the steps of a very important and highly secret project. As you listen intently, you are told what that project is and how important its completed outcome is. You are also told that because you have the gift of mind and thought you hold the key to putting all the appropriate pieces in their correct order and sequence to bring about something tangible and concrete. A spiral stairway is placed centrally in the room and each step is a beautiful shade of blue marble. As you near the top you see that there is a violet colored door just ahead and you step through.

You find yourself in what appears to be a small room. Its walls change in color from violet to indigo making you unsure of what color you are really seeing. You also notice that what appeared to be a solid wall just in front of you is actually an opening to what appears to be a corridor. As you move closer, you see that the hall is dark amber in color and seems to stretch upwards. You begin to walk along this amber colored hallway. There is a slight incline as you walk and you feel the exhilaration of exertion of effort at moving towards your destination.

As you move along the amber color gives way to a dark orange glow and you find yourself stepping into a room. You take notice that there is a pool, spherical in shape, in the center of the room and its water casts a shimmering reflection mirrored back on russet-colored glass walls. You now see that this room has eight walls; each a prism of gold-flecked light dancing on their crystalline like surface from the pool's reflection. Just near the edge of the pool is a chair upon which you are to sit. The chair is a deep purple, the color of a rare and beautiful amethyst and it is covered in rich velvet cloth and is cool and comfortable to sit on. You sit down and begin to look more closely at your surroundings before you begin the task at hand. The ceiling and floor of the room are a rich orange in color and the floor of the pool glows with orange infused light. As your eyes scan the eight walls you think on the significance of this number, the lemniscates and its ribbon of eternity. You come to the realization that your thought process is similar in nature with each thought feeding the other; each coming full circle then converging and crossing before moving onto the next phase of idea. As you begin to become one with your thoughts and mind's inspiration your gaze settles on the pool of waters in front of you. As you look onto its surface your consciousness flows gently into the small waves of almost imperceptible movement on the water's surface. You become as the waters, placid yet full of potential for shape and form. The orange colored sides and the floor of the pool are seen not only as the strength and support for the waters, but also the container or vessel holding this place of potential for movement of current. You become aware of yourself and your mind as being similarly a container for the downpour of mingling of celestial waters of mind and the current of charged inspiration. Sit for a moment in this space and with this awareness of connection between the minds of logic and Higher Reason. Allow the answers to the project you have been given to flow within this birthing place of mind. Be open and welcoming of each step as it is presented. With each new thought comes the awareness that you and your physical being are the third element of potential that produces the current of electrical charge that lights the path towards manifestation. Continue to sit in this place of reflective thought until you have completed as much of the bits and pieces of the project as you are able. The last vital piece of information to complete your project comes easily and smoothly and satisfied with your efforts, you stand and walk towards the door to share your work with your guide. As you turn to take one last look at the pool you feel that there is one more thought that should be added; one more idea that would really make this project viable. Just as quickly as that thought came, you dismiss the idea, rationalizing that you had spent quite long enough here and that your work was more than sufficient.

You see the opening to the corridor through which you entered and the amber colored walls leading the way back to the room where you met your guide. You move more easily on the descent downwards and with each step the excitement about sharing your completed project builds as you continue on. You step back into the small violet colored room and again have the impression that what you see within this room is not always as it seems, so you are both delighted and surprised when you realize that the shadowy silhouette in the corner begins to move towards you and is your guide. Momentarily startled by seeing him in this room rather than where you originally had your meeting your excitement becomes hesitation at the thought of letting go of your work sooner than planned. Thoughts of doubt and the merit of your work begin to fill your mind and as he greets you, asking you to share what you have formulated as plan and design you hesitate for a brief moment. The first few sentences uttered very softly and tentatively. As you move through your description and explanation you see that he appears pleased with the results and begin to speak with more ease and assertiveness.

You are certain now that your work was right on the mark and that much praise will be given for your brilliant plans. Your guide speaks and says that although you have done quite a good job, there is still much more that could and needs to be added before these steps can be brought into manifest form. You are gently told to take this unfinished project home with you and to sleep on it for a few nights and then look at its components with a fresh mind and clear head each of the mornings on awakening. You are also told to rethink a particular step in the process and to be sure not to allow the illusion of preconceived notions about its importance to the finished project get the best of you. Your guide sees that you are disappointed with his response and assures you that every great idea, project or object of manifest form has had many layers of thought, emotion, desire and energy laid upon it. That hours and millennia have been spent in the production of one single thread of life and that only those that have passed the test and filters of illusory success versus pure inspiration come to the place of the physical realm. Hearing these words sets your mind at ease and you are anxious to continue your work on this most important project. You thank your guide and walk towards the spiral stairway to begin your return home.

You begin your decent; each step of the stairway a beautiful shade of blue marble and on this journey downward, you now see that etched into each of the steps is a symbol. You make note of what this symbol is, feeling that it is key in some way to the continued work on your project. Your feet touch lightly onto the landing and you are once again in the office. The smell of earth now fragrant and full, and the tones and shades of the room more vital and enlivened looking. Stepping out of the office and entering the lobby everything seems to have more clarity and you have a greater sense of the work, planning, effort and thought that went into the design of this beautiful building. Feeling very much at home and part of this process of thought and manifest reality, you move through the revolving doors and out into the brilliance of a sunlit day.

You stand taking in the fullness and strength of the Sun and with each breath focus your awareness back to the rhythm of your breath and the rise and fall of your chest. Become aware of the physicality of where you are sitting or laying; your body pressed against cushion, chair or floor.

And when you are ready, gently flutter your eyes open

The Sphere of Netzach: The Emerald Rooms

Turn your focus and attention to your breath. Allow your consciousness to move with the rise and fall of your chest and the filling and release of the lungs. Continue in this manner for several breaths; allowing each to become softer, smoother and slower. With each breath your physical body appears to lighten and your center of consciousness floats upwards towards the inner eye. You feel enveloped by the mist of transition between the Physical and Astral.

As you continue to breathe in a relaxed manner, you become aware of yourself standing in the center of an elegantly lit jewelry store. All around you are cabinets of the finest most aromatic woods and display cases transparent with clear clean glass holding the most opulent and beautiful jewelry, trinkets and gifts you could imagine. The scene is one of utter luxury. Crystal and gold chandeliers hang from finely mural painted ceilings and the air is fragrant and wonderfully scented with sandalwood. Gemstones sparkle from velvet-lined cases and there is a dignified calm and serene quiet that fills the vast room.

As you move past each case you feel an intense desire to own one of these cherished and rare gems. You imagine the sensuality of a string of diamonds encircling your neck or the cool caress of a liquid platinum bracelet entwined around your wrist. As these thoughts stir within you, your attention is drawn to a rather large emerald resting on a pewter colored velvet swatch. There is no setting, just a beautifully multi-faceted stone. On closer inspection, the stone appears oddly shaped and slightly imbalanced despite the appearance initially of regular rectangular edges.

You ask to have the stone removed so that you may have a closer look. As soon as it is taking from the case and set on the display cloth you feel drawn to it. As you stare more deeply into the facets of its center you find that a myriad of sensations comes over you.

You slowly feel yourself drawn into the very heart of the stone and find yourself in the midst of seven clearly etched paths. These are the facets within the stone itself.

The emerald green floods your senses and the creative urge within you opens in response to the breathtaking beauty that surrounds you. As you move towards one of the paths you become aware of the smell of briny sea. You move along this faceted corridor and soon find yourself standing at the edge of the sea. There are trees near the water's edge and the surface begins to bubble with motion. As you stand in anticipation of what may lay beneath the ocean's surface, the top of a beautiful young woman's head emerges. Her hair is the color of spun gold and before you can comprehend what is taking place she emerges; unclothed, beautiful of form and face standing atop a giant clamshell. You know from pictures you have seen that this is Venus. Young and the embodiment of love and beauty. You stand for a moment longer, mesmerized by her beauty, but also curious as to what other mysteries the other corridors may hold.

As these thoughts echo within your mind, you become aware of tones and sounds coming from one of the other corridors. As you move towards its entrance and begin walking down the path, the sounds become louder, more potent and fuller in quality. When you reach the inner chamber of this corridor you see that there are seven figures, cloaked in shadowy silhouette that stand at each of the edges of this seven sided room. Each in turn tones a specific sound and the dynamics of vibration and resonance seem to reach your very core. You are deeply moved at the beauty of the harmonics of these sounds and you feel as though time has ceased; each tone capturing and reweaving its own time signature on your experience. As you stand centrally, bathing in the luxurious sounds, you begin to discern what the tones represent. Each is a Bija, a sacred sound that holds the energy of what it represents. As the sound becomes more identifiable you realize that each is a Bija related to one of the seven chakras. Lam-Vam-Ram-Yam-Ham-Om- Om and then, silence. You feel your body relaxing and the energy within you awakens. You feel revitalized, renewed and each repetition connects you more deeply to your thinking self and your feeling self. You stand for several minutes in the echo of this resonance and then slowly turn to leave feeling refreshed.

As the sounds begin to fade you start down the third corridor. The smell of paint and turpentine, linseed oil and freshly stretched canvas fills your nostrils and you soon emerge into a brightly sunlit room where an artist is standing engrossed in her work. The painting that stands on the easel is abstract in design. Colors flow one to the other- emerald green- amber- yellowish green and olive with sparkling gold flecks. She is so totally absorbed by her painting that she does not notice you have entered the room. You stand quietly in a corner taking in each stroke of the brush as if it were your own creation. You can feel the energy of passion about her work and the yearning to create something of permanence that may be enjoyed by all. You stand as silent observer and feel the reverence this artist feels for her craft. You can imagine what images were created in the mind as a result of the deep yearning for expression of her emotional self and this is the product of that merging and collaboration. This is a place of inspiration and although you would find much pleasure in remaining in this place of creativity, more awaits your exploration.

You move along the corridor out of the artist's hall and walk towards another unexplored corridor. This hall seems to be darkening as you move along and for a moment you hesitate to continue, fearful of what may lay ahead. Fear soon gives way to curiosity and you realize that you have stepped into the chamber of another facet. The space is cold and dark and weightlessness carries you upwards. You are in the deepest and darkest of space. As you look around you see that there are several sparkling stars in the velvet of this skyscape. From your studies as a young student you recognize a cluster of stars just ahead that form the Pleiades. This formation is known as the Seven Sisters and myths abound around the formation these stars make. As you muse on these myths you realize that you are moving forward towards the center of these stars. You feel the energy around you and are awestruck by the number, radiance and beauty of this stellar landscape. You are reminded of Lord Tennyson's quote about the Pleiades, "Many a night I saw the Pleiades, rising thro' the mellow shade, Glitter like a swarm of fireflies tangled in a silver braid." As you allow these words to move through your being heaviness begins to settle in and you realize that you have returned to the crystalline floor and chamber once again. The Night sky has very quickly moved from your surrounding and you begin to move out of the room towards the other remaining corridors.

As you reach the point of pathways, you decide to follow one in which you can see very dimly the glowing of a light. There are muffled voices that you hear as you move forward and you find yourself in the lamp lit kitchen of a small and cozy kitchen. A father and his daughter are sitting at a small wooden kitchen table in the center of the room. You hear the father say to her that she is only 10, and although she is considered gifted mathematically, she should not be so hard on herself as these problems are very difficult. You see the frustration on the young girl's face as she puzzles though the college level homework assignment. You see the expression and sense the great love and pride this father has for her, this being the only gift of support he may offer as the multi-stepped problem is well beyond the skills of his analytical mind. This sense of great and unconditional love overwhelms you and your heart pours out to their combined efforts. "Eureka", the girl exclaims as the answer is committed to paper and father and daughter hug each other. The one providing the love and the other providing the intellect. Problem solved. Feeling as though you are intruding on this intimate moment you make your way down the corridor and stand for a moment in the central chamber. Each of your experiences thus far has given you a different perspective on how the emotions and the mind work in harmony with one another. Two more corridors lay ahead and you move towards the one at the right.

As soon as you step into the entryway the fragrance of a rose garden fills your senses. In anticipation of what beautiful flora may await you run down the corridor only to find that there is only one rose standing in a small finely etched crystal vase on a green dais. You look around convinced that there must be several vases that have been carefully hidden within the room, for no single rose could have emitted such a powerful aroma. Each corner of the room is well lit and it is soon clear that there are no other flowers.
As you approach this rose, you are entranced by the vibrancy of the red petals. Each petal is perfectly shaped and each is placed in perfect accord and symmetry to the other. The rose is open just enough to see the delicate center and the edges of each petal are of the faintest pink. The fragrance is heady and rich, finer and more pure than any flower you have ever smelled. Everything about this rose speaks of beauty, of refinement of form, grace of shape and perfection in symmetry. You stand mesmerized by its perfection and you are almost brought to tears in being able to see something of such rare form. You admire for several more seconds and then begin to move away, realizing that you could easily become lost in gazing at this flower. You slowly and reluctantly move back towards the center chamber and once arriving begin your journey down the final corridor.

As you move more deeply into this facet, you see that the corridor is becoming more lit as you travel forward. Just as you step into the center of this final room, a flash of brilliant light fills the room. It disperses and you see that the source is a golden lamp that has been placed centrally on the floor. As you move slightly closer, the glow within the lamp begins to brighten and after a slow crescendo of increase, another burst of brilliant light fills the room. You move back a bit and take notice that this pattern seems to be repeating in a rhythmic and regular fashion. The slow increase, the brilliant light and the slow fade back to a gentle glow. Instinctively you know that this is also the pattern of the light within you. The energy that builds slowly through the accumulated experiences of heart. The culmination of that building to a place of illumination and great light as the realization or mind grasps the mysteries that have been given. And, the gentle fade back to the place of a warm glow within, as each experience is assimilation, integrated and processed anew. You begin your walk back to the central room and feel the glow of this lamp emanating from you.

You stand in the center of the main chamber. Each of the seven facets and their corridors flooding through you as experiences you will take with you and carry always close to your heart. You breathe deeply and recall the smell of paint and canvas, sea foam and a rose so intoxicating that you feared you would not leave. You close your eyes and visions of a star lit night, and challenging analytical problems solved form a slide show on your inner screen. Sounds echo back of tones so refined that the essence of your being was shaken. All of these senses respond and the inner chamber begins to fade returning you to the place of looking down at this rare gem. The facets are more clearly indicated now and the emerald green is rich and luxurious, almost bursting with life. There is no longer any desire to possess this jewel for you know that the facets and layers of your experiences are now part of your inner self. You will carry this jewel of great price wherever you go and the inner lamp of the mysteries will glow for all who have the sight of wisdom to see.

Return your awareness to your breath. Allow the image of this emerald to fade slowly and with each breath bring your awareness back to the rhythm of your breath and the rise and fall of your chest. Become aware of the physicality of where you are sitting or laying; your body pressed against cushion, chair or floor.

And when you are ready, gently flutter your eyes open

The Sphere of Tiphareth: The Heart of the Sun

Turn your focus and attention to your breath. Allow your consciousness to move with the rise and fall of your chest and the filling and release of the lungs. Continue in this manner for several breaths; allowing each to become softer, smoother and slower. With each breath your physical body appears to lighten and your center of consciousness floats upwards towards the inner eye. You feel enveloped by the mist of transition between the Physical and Astral.

As you continue to breathe in a relaxed manner, you find yourself sitting on a beautiful sandy beach. The sun is shining brightly overhead and the day is warm, with air fragrant from sea and salt and life within. All around you are surrounded by expanse of area. The beach stretches long and deep behind you and the ocean's water merges into brilliantly lit sky long and far ahead. The water is so clear that from your vantage point on the beach you would swear that you could see the mirrored reflection of the Sun in its entirety reflected on its surface.

You take some time to languish in the sensation of warm sand between naked toes and the warmth of the sun on your body and face. Time seems to slow and you feel as though you are held within a still point of space that is both ripe and full with possibilities as well as ever changing and transforming at a speed that is incomprehensible. As this feeling begins to strengthen you become aware that the boundaries between earth, ocean and sky seem to be blending and fading in distinction. It is as though all is moving inwards dynamically and magnetically as the varied energies are drawn towards a center point. As this feeling moves through your being you close your eyes and gently lean back into the softness of the sand beneath. You expect to feel the weight of sand pressing lightly against the back of your body and are surprised when you seem to be simply floating, held in a gentle swirling energy of light and heat and fluid. The feeling is not in the least unpleasant, but rather, exhilarating and the center core of your body seems to respond and expand in a flurry of gentle butterfly-like sensation that announces the awakening of your own energetic center.

Instinctively, you open your eyes and realize that you have unknowingly and without conscious effort moved to an upright position. There is only the brilliance of Light upon which you appear to be standing and you realize that you are completely enveloped in the honey golden glow of this light. It is as though you have stepped into the very core of the sun, but unlike the physical sun to which your earthly realm is accustomed, the intensity and heat of its flame is tempered. As you stand breathing in all that you are experiencing you feel the desire to move deeper into the center of this warmth. You are aware of a sensation similar to walking through gently moving water as you move ahead. You imagine that this is what it would feel like to move through liquid honey, a gentle resistance, but fragrant and warm. It is as though you are being drawn towards a deeper core guided by the strengthening of your own central core of energy that you feel midway between your solar plexus and heart chakras.

As you move deeper within the center you begin to see a swirling pool of color faintly ahead. You can make out streams of red, sky blue, green, violet, grey, black and orange and within the very center a pure crystalline stream of white light. As you move closer there is less distinction between each of the colors, yet within the violet you can see the fine threads of red diluted by blue and white. Within the grey you can distinguish the streams of pure white and the giving way of the jet-black. Each retains a certain level of individuality but is also part of the mass and volume that is the combination of all of the colors.

Moving closer still, you see that what appeared to be only a drawing in is also a release back from whence each stream of color originated. There is a pulsing of receipt and return that you feel echoing within your own being and you are reminded of the work of your physical heart in receiving what needs purification and cleansing and then the necessary release back through vein and artery to sustain life in its enriched form.

This is as close as you may get to the center for now, as the rush and wave of energy is not one you could easily navigate. Even from the place where you are standing, which is still a great distance away and still further than you can comprehend, you become increasingly aware of the power of this place. The sheer strength and energy contained and generated. You remember from a place deep within and long ago that this is the point of threshold and Gateway that only a few have completely passed through in their place of devotion and dedication to the Great Work and humanity.

This is not your challenge to take up, for you have much work that must be completed and shared that can only be achieved in the physical realm and the physical incarnation of which you are vitally a part. You stand in silence and in awe of what lay before you and you have a sense of the diversity of energy, form, color and essence that swirl and undulate before you. Take a moment to just simply be in this place. Express gratitude for the experience you have had and the deepened perspective this place of power has offered.

It is now time to return to the outer world. You turn and begin your journey back along the path you created. As you move away from the center point the sense of color fades and you find yourself once again surrounded by brightening golden light. You continue to slowly move through the honey colored warmth and fall into a sleepy rhythm of step that once again finds you in a position of laying back into warm thick liquid. You close your eyes for a moment, and the images of the swirling colored energy fill your inner screen. You feel a calm sense of being and a connection to all of life that you had not previously experienced. As you think on your experience, you sense the brightness of light and heat and warmth on your face and body. This is the gift of the physical sun. The sounds of waves and ocean and the grittiness of sand flood back into your sensory fields and you open your eyes to once again gaze out at the waters and the beach on which you are now laying. You rise to stand and drink in the beauty around you. The reflection of the sun on shimmering water now has new insight and a deeper message for you. This is the heart and sustainer of all life renewed, transformed, quickened and birthed. Its energy flows through everything and its nature of balance and synthesis transforms all that pass through its center. You have seen one part of the mystery and gnosis that lies within the spiritual sun. It is the great connector of the physical and the Gateway to the Divine. It is the reflection of the All and its grace quickens the life force within.

Allow these words to fill your mind. Each word guiding you back to the awareness of your breath. Allow the image of this sunlit beach to gently fade. Each breath bringing you back to the rhythm of your breath and the rise and fall of your chest. Become aware of the physicality of where you are sitting or laying; your body pressed against cushion, chair or floor.

And when you are ready, gently flutter your eyes open

The Sphere of Geburah: The Phoenix

Turn your focus and attention to your breath. Allow your consciousness to move with the rise and fall of your chest and the filling and release of the lungs. Continue in this manner for several breaths; allowing each to become softer, smoother and slower. With each breath your physical body appears to lighten and your center of consciousness floats upwards towards the inner eye. You feel enveloped by the mist of transition between the Physical and Astral.

As this veil thins and dissipates you see your physical self standing in the center of a chamber that is lit and encircled by a perimeter of scarlet flame. This is the Temple of Release and Transformation and within the confines of this circle of flame you may release and burn away all that restricts, binds, hinders or blocks your way towards personal spiritual growth.

As you stand centrally in this room, focus your will and intent on what you wish to shed so that you may truly see the magickal SELF of Power that you are. Allow each of the hindrances and blockages you feel are keeping you from your highest good to take shape and form. As each reaches the apex of its shape and power you see and feel each falling away from you like discarded bits of ash, burnt off and no longer holding any negative power over you. As the pile that is these unproductive energies grows, you see that they begin to rise upwards creating a veil of blue flame just a few feet in front of you. Continue to feed and fuel this veil with all that needs shedding and release. As the veil intensifies, thickens and reaches upward you are aware of the heat and energy that is projected from its core. Make note of how this energy serves to either repel or draw you towards it. This is the magnetic affect of the Power of Fire. The Power of Will. The Power of Transmutation and Transformation. When you feel the veil has reached its peak of potency, take a deep breath of strength and courage and step through the wall of flame.

You emerge on the other side and find yourself in a cool, luminescent white landscape of the astral plane of manifestation and creation. Allow your inner sight to adjust to this totally white terrain. Give pause to moving forward; just simply stand enveloped by this brilliant light in contrast to the blue veil from which you emerged. The matter underfoot gives ever so slightly as you move forward and what appears as solid you can now see to be living matter, a fluid sea of matter awaiting form and shape by use of your Will and Intent.

Standing in this white astral plane, shift the focus of your inner eye to a space at your feet a few feet in front of you and form in your mind the intent and will to give form to your transformed self. This persona is bourne from release to flame, and release of those things that have caused you lack and despair. You see yourself rising from the discarded ash and emerging strong and renewed. Allow yourself to fully connect with and integrate the feelings of strength and enlivenment that exude from this vision. Take in all of the experience of standing in this place of power; of you rising like the phoenix, reborn and free from what has chained you.

Now, turn your awareness to the space around you. You see that the white has now changed to reflect color and landscape. This is the space that is the reality of your physical being. Ad, you are standing strong and centered in this space. Take a look around and more fully see what is presented to you. Allow your thoughts to open to the message of this new surrounding and to what place you have in it and how it may help or reflect your transformed Power of Self and Will. This place is the gift and lesson of the strength and power you hold within. The message of the Phoenix reborn from what it has consumed and ready to take flight. The mere brush of the tips of its wings affecting change and new growth. This is your place of change and transformation. The essence of the Power within. Drink in the wisdom of that knowledge and feel the heat of its transformation. Open and accepting, heed whatever else may arise. There are lessons here of coping and strategies of maintaining a space of clarity, free from the thoughts that bind and hold you. Listen to what is being said in the silence.

You have received all that is needed at this time. Take a last look around. Feel the warmth of your being energized and recharged. Close your inner eyes and feel yourself enveloped in the veil of transition between the Physical and Astral world.

The veils of transformation and all they contain gently fade from your sight and you begin the descent back into your physical state of being and the room and space in which you began this pathworking. Return to awareness of the rhythm of your breath and the rise and fall of your chest. Become aware of the physicality of where you are sitting or laying; your body pressed against cushion, chair or floor.

And when you are ready, gently flutter your eyes open

The Sphere of Chesed: The Foundation

This pathworking is based upon the ritual experience within the Sphere of Chesed for the Assembly of the Sacred Wheel's Climbing The Tree weekend (Oct. 2009) as crafted by Jim Welch, H.P (Troupe of the Starry Door) and Robin Fennelly, HPs. (Oak and Willow)

Turn your focus and attention to your breath. Allow your consciousness to move with the rise and fall of your chest and the filling and release of the lungs. Continue in this manner for several breaths; allowing each to become softer, smoother and slower. With each breath your physical body appears to lighten and your center of consciousness floats upwards towards the inner eye. You feel enveloped by the mist of transition between the Physical and Astral. As this veil thins you see before you a cobalt blue double door. The door is wood and ornately carved with markings that denote royalty is held behind these closed doors. You reach out and push against the doors and find yourself at the threshold of a throne room.

In the front of the room, just ahead is an ornately carved throne of gold and dark wood. The room is square in shape and the walls are painted a beautiful shade of blue. You look upwards and the ceiling is made of crystal clear glass and looks out to beautiful clear blue sky. The floor is constructed of 4-sided tiles of azure with flecks of gold glistening back. There is a feeling of security and great power held within this place.

Directly in front of the throne, and centrally placed is a four-sided altar placed juxtaposed to each of the connecting corners of the walls of the room. It is draped with four colored cloths of the finest materials. Each layered one on the other and slightly smaller creating a multi-layered palette of deep violet, cobalt blue, deep purple and azure blue. You recognize these colors as being the Four Worlds of the sphere of Chesed and you marvel at their beauty when all are combined, yet remaining singular in design.

Each quarter end of the altar contains 4 beautifully decorated and distinctly different wooden cubes.

As you look up from the altar you now see that there is a figure seated on the throne. The figure gestures to you to come forward and as you approach you see it is a male figure. He is dressed in royal blue and purple robes and wears a glistening gold crown upon his head. His smile is one of welcoming and you sense a gentleness as well as great power about his persona. His eyes glisten as they come to rest upon your face and he directs to come sit on the carpeted stair beside him. As he takes your hand in his you feel a flood of overwhelming compassion pour out and his words indicate that he understands the energy and effort you have put into arriving finally at this place of grandeur.

"Your journey had been arduous and long and you now must integrate and bring those things within to a place of greater foundation. All you need lay within your grasp and all parts of your Higher Self await renewal and transformation." The words engulf you in a gentle embrace of loving-kindness. He continues, " I sit upon this throne you see before you. Is it not grand? Is it not beautiful and worthy of my kingship?". You nod in agreement and he leans in closer to you and says, "This throne is contained within you. You hold the power and magnificence of its weight and meaning within the core of your Divine Self. You have only to acknowledge and claim it."

The words move through you and awaken the memory of what seemed a distant dream. You know that these are words of truth and great power and you question the worthiness of your acquisition. The king rises and draws you up to your feet. He says, "Come walk with me through my kingdom and see what is held within the expanse of my energy."

You take a few steps and suddenly are transported to the edge of a beautiful blue ocean. You feel the spray of water on your face and hear the crashing of waves. You look over the great expanse and see only the edge of horizon meeting waterline and marvel at the beauty of this place. " The oceans are my domain. The mysteries of their depths and the life that they hold are all within my scope. I could command that they rise in honor of my status, but that would serve no purpose. I could draw all of the life that is contained to heed my command, but that would disrupt the natural order of things, and cause chaos where there should be balance and mercy."

Again, these words stir something within me that lay buried, but was once the code of my course. "Come child" and with these words just barely finished you are standing at the summit of what appears to be the tallest mountain you could imagine. You seem to be able to just reach up and touch the clouds and brilliant blue of the sky in one extension of your arm. As you look down, everything appears miniature is perspective. You have the vantage of sight of an eagle soaring high above in this lofty realm.

"All you see spread before you is my domain. The winds and the sky bow to my command and the mystery of the starry heavens fills my stores of knowledge. From this place of great height I can see all that lays below and the harmony and balance of order is displayed as a map below." These words are captured on the breeze of your imagination and float like wisps of cool air around you.

'You take a deep breath in filling your lungs with the cool clean air and as you exhale you find yourself once again in the throne room, standing in front of the altar. The King points to the cubes that are placed within each of the quarters and directs you to place them in whatever fashion and pattern you wish in the center of the altar table. You are told that this pattern reflects your understanding of what you have been shown and the foundation or base upon which you will begin to build your connection and memory of these gifts of the Divine. You are reminded to draw upon your understanding and experience of the previous spheres you have studied from Malkuth to Chesed.

Take a moment to look at each of the cubes. Inspect and feel its weight, color and size. Plan carefully and open yourself to your inner knowing to act as guide as you place each block in whatever fashion you are inspired.

Go within and seek guidance about what areas of your physical life are in need of more mercy and what Spiritual goals need more compassion and patience to bring to fruition; these are the bases from which you grow. You move with deliberation and confidence. Each cube placed seems to reveal yet another layer of memory and form as you proceed. As you place the last cube in place you step back smiling and content with the structure you have created.

The King, pauses for a moment, observes and then asks you to describe to him what meaning is held within the creation you have constructed. How this fits into your understanding of what has been shown to you and how you will use this as base for future movement. He listens with rapt attention and interest as you speak and a gentle smile of pride in your efforts moves across his face.

"You have done well, and have learned much. Do not forget what you have created here. Do not allow yourself to slip back into the slumber of inertia and overindulgence. Take what you have learned, build upon it and use it to share and give back to others. Serve as both the inspiration and the one who is continually inspired by the generosity that abounds in a heart that is filled with Divine Love. And, as you walk this path of service, do so in joy and in reverence for those who join you; for that is the true abundance that may be received from one who gives without condition."

As the last of his words sounds forth, you are bathed in the radiance of Divine Love. You feel at one with all of life and are ready to cross into a new way of being.

As you stand centrally looking at your construct and taking in the energy of the King's words, a sound of toning fills the room. This sacred tone crescendos and you feel the response of your chakras. This enlivened energy moves through your entire being. The toning continues for a few minutes more and as it begins to fade and you open your eyes you see that you are once again alone in the throne room. The King is no longer present and the central altar that held your creation is no longer in sight.

There is a faint glow around the edge of the double doorway and you know that it is time to return to your daily activities and normal state of being. You move towards the doors, take one last look around and gently push them open, stepping through to a dense blue mist. This is the veil of transition and juncture between your visioning and the manifest world. You feel yourself enveloped in the veil of transition between the Physical and Astral world.

The veils of transformation and all they contain gently fade from your sight and you begin the descent back into your physical state of being and the room and space in which you began this pathworking. Return to awareness of the rhythm of your breath and the rise and fall of your chest. Become aware of the physicality of where you are sitting or laying; your body pressed against cushion, chair or floor.

And when you are ready, gently flutter your eyes open

The Sphere of Binah: The Cradle of Life

Turn your focus and attention to your breath. Allow your consciousness to move with the rise and fall of your chest and the filling and release of the lungs. Continue in this manner for several breaths; allowing each to become softer, smoother and slower. With each breath your physical body appears to lighten and your center of consciousness floats upwards towards the inner eye. You feel enveloped by the mist of transition between the Physical and Astral. As this veil thins you see before you a black door. The door is a matte finish and you are not quite sure what material it has been made from. It is both liquid and solid in feel. You reach out and push against the door and find yourself stepping into what appears to be dense and thick blackness.

You take a deep breath and muster all of your courage and any fears you may have leave just as quickly as they may have come as you gently exhale. You move forward and are surprised to feel a buoyant softness beneath your feet. It moves in rhythm with your step, giving way slightly with each footfall, but nonetheless gently supporting your weight. You are in a complete state of trusting your instinct as the darkness is so pervasive you cannot see your outstretched hand in front of you.

You take a few more steps; unsure of which direction you are actually traveling and take note that this place has a feeling of being non-linear in nature. You are sure that it is multi-dimensional, as well; which makes finding your bearings next to impossible. Your sensibilities try to grab onto the control of knowing the direction in which you are moving, but each time the knowledge slips through your grasp of mind. Weary from thinking on this, you decide to simply rest and stop. Gently you lower yourself into what now seems to be a pool of thick liquid. Funny, but it did not feel that way as you were walking, so you are surprised at this new turn of events.

The liquid barely covers your legs as you sit, so you feel comfortable resting here for a bit. Take a few moments and sit quietly. Allow whatever thoughts or images that wish to present themselves to you to come easily; not lingering or dwelling too long on any. Be in this space of darkness for as long as you wish and when you feel ready gently rise, for it is now time to move on and deeper into this womb of darkness. You take a few steps forward and become aware of a rhythmic pulse of sound. It reminds you of the gentle inhale and exhale of breath and the sound of the air as it fills lungs and gives life and then is released back into the atmosphere.

You find that as the sound increases, your rhythm of breath is mirroring each dynamic pulse that surrounds you. You breathe gently and easily, each breath folding into the pace that surrounds you. You are breathing the life of the universe. You are inhaling the first swirl of the void and breathing out the stars, planets, form and force. You are at once creator and co-creator. Continue to breathe in this manner for several more minutes. After a time you once again find you have returned to your own pace and rhythm of breath.

Suddenly, there is a flash of blinding light that startles you. The blackness has held you as a mother holds her child close to her breast. You look upwards towards the origin of this Light and the star light of the Great Mother's loving gaze stares down at you, her most precious creation and you feel an overwhelming sense of love and protection. A deep gnosis of all space and time envelopes and encompasses every part of your being. You drink in this light hungrily. She closes her eyes and you lean back into the embrace and gentle support of the velvety blackness. Tiny particles of light flicker about you and the darkness feels warm and alive around you. The body of the Mother holds you closely in her embrace. Rest for some time in the space of these loving energies. Allow every cell of your being to be open to receiving this gift of great love, understanding and deep knowing. Be held in the profound silence and the tender care of SHE who gave you life. Be still. Simply be at one with this primal creatrix.

You have received all that is needed at this time. You feel loved, at peace, inspired and renewed. You feel yourself being gently released from her embrace and as the darkness thins you can see the outline of the door through which you came just ahead. As you move towards it, you know that the feelings and experience of this journey are there for you always. You have but to breathe into the energy of the Universe to connect with your First Mother. Her love surrounds you and her gaze flows through the moonlit nights and the stars that feel the sky above.

There is a faint glow around the edge of the doorway, so it is easy to see where it is and you know that it is time to return to your daily activities and normal state of being. You move towards the door and gently push it open, stepping through to a dense blue mist. This is the veil of transition and juncture between your visioning and the manifest world. You feel yourself enveloped in the veil of transition between the Physical and Astral world.

The veils of transformation and all they contain gently fade from sight and you begin the descent back into your physical state of being and the room and space in which you began this pathworking. Return to awareness of the rhythm of your breath and the rise and fall of your chest. Become aware of the physicality of where you are sitting or laying; your body pressed against cushion, chair or floor.

And when you are ready, gently flutter your eyes open

The Sphere of Chokmah: The Wheel of the Cosmos

Turn your focus and attention to your breath. Allow the space of your consciousness to move with the rise and fall of your chest and the filling and release of the lungs. Continue in this manner for several breaths; allowing each to become softer, smoother and slower. With each breath your physical body appears to become lighter and your center of consciousness floats upwards towards the inner eye. You feel enveloped by the mist of transition between the Physical and Astral.

As this veil thins you step through a veil of dark blue mist and find yourself standing centrally in a circular room. As you look around you see that this space opens out to a star lit night sky. The velvety blackness above holds a twinkling of starry light that fills the panoramic view above. The walls encircle you and are of a deep bluish purple. As your eyes adjust to this room you notice an archway just ahead of you. It glows a deep blood red in color and you are intrigued by what may lay through the archway.

♈ You step forward and pass easily through the archway stepping through the glyph of Aries and out into a room that is vibrantly colored red. You see the astrological sigil of Aries and feel a surge of youthful exuberant energy wash over you. There is a table placed centrally with a variety of objects placed upon it and you feel the overwhelming desire to explore these items. You gingerly pick up each object, looking carefully at it and seeing that some are similar in use. You are overwhelmed by the urge to create something new that will be the summation of what you have selected. Having completed this task, you look around eager for someone to see what you have done. For another who will take notice of what you have achieved. Seeing that no one is there you dismantle your project and set to work creating something new. You are sure that this time, someone will appear that you may share this wonderful

235

invention with. Again you are left alone with this new object and just as you are begin to feel a bit of frustration that your efforts have gone unnoticed you see another archway off to the side. There is a glow of soft green light and you immediately feel compelled to step through.

♉ As soon as you step into this room you notice the powerful glyph of Taurus. You also notice that it is a bit more difficult to move quickly in this space. It is as though you have become fixed or rooted in the spot on which you are standing and although you wish to move forward there is a bit of hesitancy as you stand your ground. The air has a heavy quality about it, and you surmise that this is more from inertia than density. It takes all your strength and energy to push through this density and you feel as though you are walking on a very windy day facing into the storm. Each step forward increases this feeling of agitation and frustration. Each step forward also makes you step with more grounded effort and with a weightiness of purpose and intent. You feel unyielding in your determination and with slow and steady progress you make your way towards the opposite end of the room. You see just ahead another archway, glowing with an orange hue. You stop for moment and now realize that in your efforts to make your way through this room, you did not take time to look at what may be contained within it. As you relax into these thoughts, the atmosphere begins to lighten in density. There is a lessening of the pressure that surrounded you and you find you are able to move quite freely now. You look around and see that the room has been decorated with items that instill a sense of family, home and comfort. There are shades of soft earthy greens and reds throughout and the overall quality is one that invites you to linger and relax. You are enticed, but know that there is more to be experienced and you move easily and more quickly towards the archway.

Ⅱ As you step through the orange glow of the Glyph of Gemini you see two perfect twins sitting having a conversation. Question, answer, and statement flash back and forth between the two at lightning speed. You feel both energized and a bit of exhaustion as your mental processes are not of this mindset and cannot keep pace with the chameleon like changes in rhythm, clarity and intonation. Books line the shelves and papers are strewn about haphazardly as though they had recently been rifled through and then carelessly left wherever they were put. You stand off to the side and observe how each of the children seems to change their mental position at will. One will agree on what statement had been made and then completely disagree about another. The other seeming to mirror every change of its twin with a steady and regulated pace. As they move around the room going from one conversation to another surrounding this book or that you sense that somehow although appearing to be two, they are actually of one mind. That the duality you are seeing is actually the mental acrobatics of a mind that shifts and moves in accord with whatever the stronger enticement lay. This is the secret of their mental agility. The sheer ability to adapt and change at will to suit the needs of the situation. Although you are excited to feel this pulse of energy and anxious to move freely, and continue keeping pace with their trail of thoughts, you notice that just ahead is another archway. This is lit with a royal purple hue and the glyph of Cancer beckons you forward drawing you in and offering rest from the frenetic energies of this space.

♋ As soon as you step through the archway the smells of the ocean and its waters permeate your senses. The fullness of moonlight reflects back from water's edge and there is a sense of stillness and anticipation as the waves gently crest and fall. You feel alive and connected to everything. Your senses are alive with sounds and sights that come in flashes of memory. Emotion wells up deep inside of you and the beauty and serenity of this place seems almost more than you can bear. As you stand in the moonlight the gentle darkness appears to give way to the rising of a brilliantly lit sun. When you look again you see that this warm glow of light is coming from another archway. You walk towards the golden light and step through the archway.

♌ Passing through the glyph of Leo, there is an intensity of heat and you find that you are standing on a desert that is scorched and parched from the heat of the Sun. In the distance you hear the low rumble of what may hold promise of a much needed thunderstorm and the strength that you feel in this place increases as the sun rises higher in the sky. You feel as though you are the center of this world and there is nothing that you cannot accomplish. The fires of passion fill your belly with desire to create, to protect and to guard well those you love. There is a primal ferocity to this feeling that you have never experienced before and you know that you would travel to the ends of the earth to safeguard those you hold dear to you. In response to this feeling, you let out a loud and deep guttural sound that comes from a place deep inside and contains more strength and courage than you imagined could be possible. The sound carries into the distance and across this wasteland and you feel in control and powerful. As these feelings move through the center of your being you notice an opening just ahead. The faint glow and colors of beautifully striated rock glisten at the entrance to the archway.

♍ As you move forward through the glyph of Virgo you step into an earth-toned decorated room that has newly polished file cabinets lining the walls. Everything is placed neatly and precisely organized. There is a sense of great detail in all that you see. A lithe beautiful woman whose age is difficult to tell immediately greets you, and with a gentle persuasive voice she asks that you describe in detail the experience of your journey thus far. You sit on one of the polished wooden chairs and begin to recount your story. As you tell all that you can remember she makes notes and promises to review them later and bind them in a richly detailed journal for you to pick up later. You feel comfortable in this place and would like to stay longer, but know there is much more to experience. As you look ahead you see the glowing light of soft green in the archway just ahead. Getting up, you thank the young woman, promise to return at a later date and walk towards the next arch.

♎ You step through the glyph of Libra into an ornate and richly decorated room filled with gold and gemstones. Around you are workbenches and expert jewelers and metal smiths crafting rings. The gold is measured precisely on scales that gleam and balance with the slightest breath of touch and after careful weighing and scrutiny for imperfections, is melted into a liquid spun of light and heat. As the mold is filled with this rare essence, gems of varying shapes and sizes are inspected and one, a rare emerald, is selected to be the main focus of the piece of jewelry. As you look around at the walls, you notice artwork that is beautiful and insightful on each of the walls. You are surrounded by luxury, beauty and harmony of mind and heart. This is not a place that is easy to leave but as you stand in the midst of all of this beauty a feeling of sadness wells up within you. You realize that this opulence is not the normal standard for most. That beauty this rare is not often enjoyed by those of limited means. You see an underlying and certain darkness about this place and as the brilliance of gold and gem dims you notice a deep red glow that is emanating from a now clearly visible archway just ahead. You turn and take in this sight one last time and step towards the energy that is beckoning you into its center.

♏ As soon as you pass through the glyph of Scorpio you are engulfed in shadow. Glimpses of light are hidden beneath what appear to be shadowy figures and although you do not feel threatened, you know this is a place of great power and deserving of care and respect as you pass through. You see that one of the walls holds a full length mirror and although you wish to leave this place as quickly as possible, curiosity takes hold and you cannot resist the temptation to glance into the mirror ever so briefly. As you move towards it with trepidation, all manner of thoughts and emotions rise up from a place deep within your core. As you stare at the reflection in the mirror, it seems to shift and change ever so slightly, almost imperceptibly. Each emotion, each deeply buried thought seems to appear etched on your face, held in the stance of your posture and staring back at you. Some are things you thought you had released long ago and others are newly formed. You are mesmerized by all that you see and when you have seen as much as you can absorb at this moment, you feel the urge to move on. You turn away from the mirror and your attention is caught by a cobalt blue veil of energy within an archway just ahead. You eagerly move forward glad to be free of this space for the time.

♐ You pass easily through the glyph of Sagittarius. Little sparks of flame lay at your feet creating a pathway through which you begin to walk. You look down and get a bit closer to one and notice that from each of the sparks a single flower appears to be in the process of blooming. As you look more closely, inspecting each along the path you see that some are viable and some wither and die as the spark goes out. Some appear to be desperately trying to take root and others never seem to catch on at all. You think of the archer, bursting with enthusiasm at the promise of hitting the center mark. The strain of arrow pressed back against bending bow and the sigh of release and effort as it is sent towards its destination. The energy of enthusiasm fills this space. The enthusiasm that turns to disappointment at those arrows shot in vain or turning to pride in accomplishment at those that hit the target. You remind yourself that a sharp eye and a steady hand can be the detriment or the success of your endeavors. You think of the times you have exerted your will in disbursed effort and the outcomes of those tiny flames of action set forth. Looking around, you realize you have walked nearly to the end of this passage, your aim clear and true, and its effort gone unnoticed in your musings. Just ahead you see the glyph of Capricorn. There is no distinguishable color beckoning you forward and you appear to be walking towards absolute darkness.

♑ Nonetheless, you persevere forward and find yourself standing at the edge of a cliff. It is evening and the darkness you saw was the velvety blackness of sky. You look downwards and see a sheer drop, very steep and not likely to be navigated in this darkness. You stand steady and still, contemplating if you should turn and go back and no sooner has that thought reached its end than a flash of brilliance lights up the night sky. You are unsure of the source, it appears to be coming from a ledge a little further above, and seems to be steady and growing in brightness. Your goal now is to reach that light and in this illuminated state you now can see there is a ledge above you. This ledge appears to connect a short distance across to another mountain that you can now see is directly opposite you. If you could reach that top ledge through the crawl space above you could pass safely to the other mountain. You begin to crawl and climb steadily up the side towards the opening just above. You realize that this side of the mountain is not as steep as you thought and there are enough ledges to maintain a strong hand and foot hold. You extend your arm, reaching upwards with all your might and are determined to accomplish this task. Each movement seems to come more easily as the determination becomes resolve. With continuous upward momentum, you finally pull yourself up and through the opening and come to rest on the connecting ledge. You can see that it is wide enough for safe passage and there is indeed another archway on the opposite side. You sit for a moment and breathe deeply, proud of the effort and proud of your achievement. You feel energized and alive and look across to see the glyph of Aquarius, lit up like a neon sign in the archway just ahead. You rise to a standing position and walk across the ledge passing through the archway.

♒ As you step into the room you feel alive with energy. The air is pulsing with it and strands of lightning like currents run down the sides of the walls. You feel inspired and enlivened and all manner of invention and idea comes rushing into your mind for your consideration. It is as though you can see everything from a greater perspective. The depths of the ocean and its life fill your vision. The canopies of the rainforest and somehow all the life that is hidden from normal sight are now revealed as though soaring above with the keen eyesight of the hawk. You see the world with fresh understanding and are optimistic about the future that could be. You see everyone and everything as part of the greater whole and now have a renewed sense of how that whole may be served and of what actions must be taken towards a future that sees life as a unified process. As you are processing all of these new experiences a feeling of great compassion and love engulfs you. You see the glyph of Pisces and know that this is what is calling forth your humane and compassionate self. There is an iridescent turquoise shimmer about the glyph of Pisces and as you step through the archway you are aware of being somehow underwater, yet able to breathe normally.

♓ You hear the cries of the whales and the sea life and before you can reach out and offer a hand of help you find yourself now on the sandy shore. You see a form just ahead of you and as you move closer you see that this beautiful creature is half fish and half woman. You feel her sorrow for both fish and human and wish to ease her suffering. You gently reach out a hand and touch her with the intent of love, compassion and care. You feel her energy strengthen with your loving touch and tears of joy and understanding fall from your eyes. It is within this place that deep connection and unconditional love are offered. As these realizations permeate your being you rise and look out onto the vastness of the ocean. The tide is returning to claim its own as you step back as the mermaid offers her thanks and you watch as she is gently carried back out to sea. As the waters move in and then recede you turn away and see the glow of the last archway that will take you back to the place of your beginning.

You step towards the entryway and pass through the arch back into the central room. In looking around it is hard to believe all the treasures that lay behind this circular wall and you think back on all the lessons that each passageway held. As you stand in this mood of reflection you see that each of the glyphs of the zodiac comes into view around the wall. Each sign held in its place of order of evolution from Aries all the way around to Pisces. They become larger and move away from the wall itself and hover in midair encircling you. Each symbol resonates with you in some way. Some, more than others, are predominant and catch your attention more fully. You stand quietly and receptive to the energy and the growing depth of gnosis that you are feeling about your place in the cosmos. This is the wisdom of your place among the stars, and the stellar blueprint that you carry within.

Gently, a mist of mother of pearl colored energy surrounds you and the astrological glyphs fade and move back into their places behind the circular wall. This is the veil of transition and juncture between your visioning and the manifest world. You feel yourself enveloped in the veil of transition between the Physical and Astral world. The veils of transformation and all they contain gently fade from your sight and you begin the descent back into your physical state of being and the room and space in which you began this pathworking. Return to awareness of the rhythm of your breath and the rise and fall of your chest. Become aware of the physicality of where you are sitting or laying: your body pressed against cushion, chair or floor.

And when you are ready, gently flutter your eyes open

The Sphere of Kether: Elevator Up!

Please Note: The colors used in this pathworking are those of Atziluth. Additionally, this pathworking is to be experienced as though you are standing within the Tree itself. Therefore the Pillar of Severity will be on your Right and the Pillar of Mercy will be on your Left.

Turn your focus and attention to your breath. Allow the space of your consciousness to move with the rise and fall of your chest and the filling and release of the lungs. Continue in this manner for several breaths; allowing each to become softer, smoother and slower. With each breath your physical body appears to become lighter and your center of consciousness floats upwards towards the inner eye. You feel enveloped by the mist of transition between the Physical and Astral. And as this veil thins you step through the swirling of white mist and find yourself standing at the end of a long, brightly lit hallway.

The floors are made of sparkling white marble and the walls are painted a luminescent white. The hall feels alive with brilliant energy and you walk towards the end of the hall stopping at a silver colored elevator just in front of you. It is lit with a bright light overhead and reflections of your image pass over the shiny silvery metal of the sides and door as you walk closer.

You push the button and the doors open into what appears to be a glass walled cabin. You take a deep breath and decide you will see where this elevator takes you. The doors close and you now see that the walls have become crystal clear and glass-like. You can see 360 degrees around and outside of the cabin. You look out into the sheer clean whiteness that begins to fade and change color.

A yellow glow of mist surrounds the enclosure, as though looking out through a filter of brilliance that appears to reflect hundreds of sunbeams. This is the sphere of Malkuth and you can see the tall full green trees, which form a canopy through which strands of early morning light gently stretch and extend to light the way. You now see just ahead of you a clearing of open field and brilliant sunlight. The noonday sun has arrived and feathery shoots of wheat fill this space. They are ochre in color with variations of tan and brown interspersed in accord with their readiness for harvest. You remember the rich woodsy smell and softness of the earth below your feet. The pulse of life that surrounded you in this space and the feeling of truly being alive and connected with all that is contained within the physical world you inhabit. You stand silently, and with awe taking in all that you see. You feel a gentle movement and realize that the enclosure is moving upwards.

As you continue on this gentle ascent, a mist of Indigo energy surrounds the enclosure. You realize that you are ascending on the Tree and this is the sphere of Yesod you are moving through. As you look out you see that you are surrounded by the velvety darkness of night. The moon is luminescent and you can almost feel the magnetic energy of its pull moving within you. You sense the resonance of the waters within your being and recognize them now as tides of time and change, ebbing and flowing in accord with the natural cycles of the moon and the stars. You feel the interconnectedness of your being and the life that is contained within the quickening and potential of this space. Dreams and images of long past memories pass through your mind and there is a feeling of rest and calm that moves over you. The energy is fluid around you and the brilliance of a moonlit night surrounds your enclosure.

You continue to rise, slowly upwards and as you turn and look out to the right you see a sphere that is veiled in a mist of Violet Purple. This is the sphere of Hod. You take notice that there is a pool, spherical in shape, in the center of the room and its water casts a shimmering reflection mirrored back on russet-colored glass walls. A prism of gold-flecked light dances on their crystalline like surface from the pool's reflection. Just near the edge of the pool is the chair upon which you sat. You remember the comfort of this chair and the work that you created as you sat in this Think Tank. You also remember the disappointment you felt after all the hard effort you had given to the assigned project. But you also remember how much more you had learned from looking at the task from a different perspective.

As these last thoughts cling foremost in your mind, you turn and look out to the left. This is the sphere of Netzach and it is veiled in a mist of Amber. You can see crystal and gold chandeliers hanging from finely mural painted ceilings and remember how the air was fragrant and wonderfully scented with sandalwood. Gemstones sparkle from velvet-lined cases; and there is an emerald and amber glow from the case that held the beautiful gemstone that revealed its innermost secrets to you. The memory of the single rose and the beauty and grace that you felt seeing it floods your senses and for a brief moment you are sure you can smell the intoxicating and heady scent that permeated the room in which it was found. You close your eyes as the scent and feelings of this sphere envelope you and can feel the gentle rise upwards of the enclosure.

As you move upwards and enter the sphere of Tiphareth a mist of clear pink rose energy surrounds the enclosure. Through the energy of this veil you begin to see a swirling pool of color and you can make out streams of red, sky blue, green, violet, gray, black and orange; and within the very center a pure crystalline stream of white light. There is a golden yellow glow to the room and you feel the energetic connection to your solar plexus. Color and flow of energy seems to be drawn towards you from every direction, swirling about the enclosure of the elevator. An ebb and flow of return and release and you remember the strength of the magnetic pull you felt as you traveled through this sphere to its solar core. The energy pulses through you and you can feel the circuit of energy it is creating. You feel energized, alive and aware of everything in more detail. This pulse of energy moves with you as you rise upwards.

You turn and look out to the right and see the sphere of Geburah veiled in a mist of Orange energy. You look into the core of this space and see in the center of the sphere an ill-defined shape and form that you remember as the unproductive energies you once released. As you observe them with clarity and intent they begin to rise upwards creating a veil of blue flame, the hottest part of the Fires of Will and transmutation. From the center-most part of this flame a flash of light emerges, the orange flames rise filling the space and from their midst the Phoenix rises once again. His wings stretched outward and open and you hear his high pitched call heeding you not to forget the power you hold within. The site is both beautiful and frightening in its power and every cell within your body vibrates with the intensity of its vibration. Although this was the harshest of your lessons, you know that it was required and perhaps the most transformative.

Unable to look any longer, you turn away, looking out to the left and are relieved to see the sphere of Chesed. It is veiled in a mist of Deep Violet and you remember the comfort you felt upon entering its realm. You see within the sphere the ornately carved throne of gold and dark wood. You look towards the upper corner of this space and see that its ceiling is made of crystal clear glass and looks out to a beautiful clear blue sky. The floor is constructed of four-sided tiles of azure with flecks of gold glistening within. Directly in front of the throne, and centrally placed is a four-sided altar placed juxtaposed to each connecting corner of the walls of the room. It is draped with four colored cloths of the finest materials. Each layered one on the other and each slightly smaller creating a multi-layered palette of deep violet, cobalt blue, deep purple and azure blue. You recognize these colors as being those of the Four Worlds of the sphere of Chesed and you marvel at their beauty when all are combined, yet remain singular in design. Each quarter end of the altar contains four beautifully decorated and distinctly different wooden cubes. You remember the lessons of this sphere and the call to memory of your own foundation and strength. You feel powerful and joyous as your ascent continues.

A mist of Lavender surrounds the enclosure as you pass through the darkness of the Abyss. As you move through this space, feelings of foreboding and a sense of being out of place in a time that is neither here nor there and in a place that is both upwards and down simultaneously flood your emotions. You are disoriented and feel as though all the joy and even the dis-ease that was felt in Geburah are shallow in comparison to the depths of sadness and loneliness that is felt in this space. Your only thoughts are the hopes that you will pass quickly and easily through this space. Quite the contrary, time seems to slow and the angst seems to become greater. And, just as you are about to scream out in sheer frustration, you remember the lesson of surrender. You remember the call to trusting and the lessons of the "Fool". You take a deep, cleansing breath and as you allow yourself to just simply 'be" open and receptive, non-resistant and assured, the enclosure begins to rise more quickly.

The veil and weight of the space seems to lift as you climb higher and the Lavender gives way to the energy of rich Crimson Red. You look out to the right and the sphere of Binah is veiled in this vibrant hue of color. As you look more closely, the red deepens and you see this as the space of darkness that is the Great Mother's womb. You hear the rhythmic pulse of sound that is Her heartbeat and it reminds you once again of the gentle inhale and exhale of breath and the sound of the air as it fills lungs and gives life and then is released back into the atmosphere. You feel safe and secure in this place of night sky, and all the feelings you had of dread and discomfort leave you with each breath. You find that as the sound increases, your rhythm of breath has become a mirror reflection of this pulse that surrounds you. You breathe gently and easily, each breath folding into the pace that surrounds you. You are breathing the life of the universe. You are inhaling the first swirl of the void and breathing out the stars, planets, form and force. You are at once creator and co-creator. You remember the comfort and ease with which you settled into the embrace of Her waters and the brilliant flash of Light as she stared back at **You**, the image of HER creation.

Feeling immense love and gratitude you turn and look out to the left. The sphere of Chokmah is veiled in a mist of pure soft blue and the glyphs of the Zodiac float circularly and centrally within the sphere. You remember walking through each of the archways and the information about yourself that was experienced. Each sign held in its place of order of evolution from Aries all the way around to Pisces. As you continue to watch, they become larger and move away from the wall; each symbol resonating with you in some way. Again you notice that some, more than others, are predominant and catch your attention more fully. You stand quietly remembering the energy and the growing depth of gnosis that you felt about your place in the cosmos. You remember that this is the wisdom of your place among the stars, and the stellar blueprint that you carry within. And, with this knowledge is the great responsibility of being merciful and just with all you encounter. You feel the motion of the ascent upwards again.

As you move upwards Light surrounds you. It brightens with each movement of the enclosure. It seems to penetrate the structure with energy that is refined and pure. All at once the space is filled with brilliance and the presence you feel in this space is unspeakable. You are filled with its energy and what was form and shape gives way to merge and blending. You realize that you are no longer within the enclosure of the elevator, and even with your eyes closed the brilliance of Light cannot be diminished. You stand strongly and fully in the space of this healing Light of creation. You open fully to the experience. The *"you"* that you have known is no longer separated from the Divinity from which you were created. Stand in this power for as long as you need.

You have received all that is needed at this time and you must return to your daily activities. Your heart is filled with gratitude and all that you thought you knew about your place in this world has changed. You are renewed, transformed and ready to embrace all of Life. As these thoughts and feelings linger and circulate within your Being, you feel yourself gently descending and you are surrounded by swirling white mist as you move downwards. This is the veil of transition and juncture between your visioning and the manifest world. You feel yourself enveloped in the veil of transition between the Physical and Astral world. You feel yourself finally coming to a rest and standstill and take a deep breath in, feeling changed and renewed by your experiences.

The veils of transformation and all they contain gently fade from your sight and you begin the remaining descent back into your physical state of being and the room and space in which you began this pathworking. Return to awareness of the rhythm of your breath and the rise and fall of your chest. Become aware of the physicality of where you are sitting or laying; your body pressed against cushion, chair or floor.

And when you are ready, gently flutter your eyes open

The Hidden Path of Da'at: The Midnight Sun

Turn your focus and attention to your breath. Allow your consciousness to move with the rise and fall of your chest and the filling and release of the lungs. Continue in this manner for several breaths; allowing each to become softer, smoother and slower. With each breath your physical body appears to lighten and your center of consciousness floats upwards towards the inner eye. You find yourself enveloped by the mist of transition between the Physical and Astral. And as this veil thins and you see before you an opening in the fabric of the space around you.

A mist of Lavender surrounds the enclosure as you pass through the darkness of the Abyss. As you move through this space, feelings of foreboding and a sense of being out of place in a time that is neither here nor there and in a place that is both upwards and down simultaneously flood your emotions. You are disoriented and feel as though all the joy and even the dis-ease that was felt in Geburah are shallow in comparison to the depths of sadness and loneliness that is felt in this space. Your only thoughts are the hopes that you will pass quickly and easily through this space. Quite the contrary, time seems to slow and the angst seems to become greater. And, just as you are about to scream out in sheer frustration, you remember the lesson of surrender. You remember the call to trusting and the lessons of the "Fool". You find that you are engulfed in shadow. Glimpses of light are hidden beneath what appear to be shadowy figures and although you do not feel threatened, you know this is a place of great power and well deserving of care and respect as you pass through.

There is no flooring under you and you have a sense of weightlessness and somehow being suspended in space. Although there are no definitive boundaries, the impression is one of being enclosed tightly in a very confining space.

You take a deep, cleansing breath and you allow yourself to simply be open, receptive and non-resistant to lesson of this Path. You take another deep breath in and ready yourself to move forward and explore this place. As soon as the sigh of exhale has passed, feelings of sadness begin to well up within you. You are fearful and now wish you had decided against entering this space. Your former resolve of being receptive and open weakening steadily as you begin to feel that you are sinking even deeper into this space of darkness.

You take another deep breath, hoping to restore your composure and as you exhale your awareness that you are alone in this space heightens. You strain to hear any sound that might point you in the direction of moving towards something; even the faintest sound of another human or animal would give you comfort. But, there is nothing, absolute and pure nothingness in this space. Your breath comes in short bursts now and the combination of sheer and utter loneliness, silence and disorientation keeps this rapid pace going.

You try to move, and find that with each step you are moving deeper into the shadowy fabric of this space, so, you decide to simply remain still. You look around and find that your eyes still have not adjusted to the darkness which now seems to be vibrating with energy, but you can neither see nor hear the source of it. You would normally have called out to the Divine or your guides to help you through this difficult passage, but you feel as though they have forsaken you as well and that in the depths of this seemingly unending well your pleas would remain unheard. This thought provokes a surge of emotional release and you begin to sob, at first quietly, then uncontrollably with louder and higher pitch.

These cries crescendo and you find that you are keening, screaming from the very base of your throat and the depths of your Soul in desperate release of this overwhelming sadness and fear. You call out to those Divine beings who are your patrons, and the only sound in return is the increased volume of your own voice. You call out to those who are family and friends. Again, the only return being the echo of your frantic cries against a surface you can neither see nor feel.

With one final exhausted effort, you pull up all of your will and courage and release a final soul filled call and as the sound issues forth from your lips, the oppressive energy around you seems to shatter and fall away. The powerful force and reverberation of the vibration wraps around you and you feel the personality that you entered this space with fall away. The ego you have carried so proudly shatters from your being and the You who entered this space moves within the spiraling of this powerful force of energy reshaping and transforming. You close your eyes and willingly surrender to this action and allow the necessary release and rebuilding of your subtle and physical forms. It seems as though time has stopped and for the briefest of moments you and all space, time and creation are one in the same.

As the energetic outpour begins to lessen around you, you gently open your eyes and looking upward see a tiny point of light above you. Although very small and far away, you can feel the intensity and radiance of this light and know it to be the reentry into the world of matter and form. As your breath slows to an even and steady pace you see that the light is growing brighter and larger as you rise on ascent towards it. Each breath pulls you closer to its light and radiance and the space around begins to brighten, the darkness and magnetic pull of the intense experience held within it slowly fading in its energy and effect on you.

You continue to rise upwards, coming to rest on a soft surface beneath your feet and completely enveloped in the brilliance of this light emanating from a space directly above you. You look at your hands and take note of a luminescent glow about them and the lower part of your body as you look downwards toward your feet.

The light begins to dim slightly and you know that there is still more of the journey you must follow through the Paths of the Higher Realm in final completion of the work done within the Dark Night. You turn to your right and see a sphere glowing black as the cosmic night and you hear the call from the Great Mother to rest in her embrace after the difficult journey you have had. You take a deep breath in, close your eyes and resolve that this next step will be taken in due time, but it is not one for now.

You gently open your eyes and see that the blue veil of transition is just a few steps in front of you. You feel yourself enveloped in the veil of transition between the Physical and Astral world. The veils of transformation and all they contain gently fade from your sight and you begin the descent back into your physical state of being and the room and space in which you began this pathworking. Return to awareness of the rhythm of your breath and the rise and fall of your chest. Become aware of the physicality of where you are sitting or laying; your body pressed against cushion, chair or floor.

And when you are ready, gently flutter your eyes open

End Thoughts

It is my hope that you have found the information contained in this book useful and that you will use these Pathworkings as Gateways to Deeper Understanding of the mysteries of the Qabalah.

Blessings of the Wisdom of the Tree of Life.... Robin

APPENDICES

APPENDIX ONE

A QUICK STUDY OF NUMBERS

0   Cycles, void, the limitless ALL, womb of creation and the Gate of the Divine

1   The singular "I", the individual, the line of continuum, energy held and gathered back to itself

2   Collaborative effort, moving beyond the "I" to "we", duality and polarity that results

3   The point of trinity or third that is created from the friction and combined effort of the two

4   Opening the point of support to a place of foundation, equanimity and force in a balanced state

5   The shield whose tip may be directed by Will to disrupt, change and set in motion

6   Doubled trinity, intersecting energies of descent and ascent, mirrored image of creative product

7   Carrying forward the lessons learned, the paths taken and the reconvening of the triune

8   The lemniscates, foundation (4) uplifted to become the container, receipt and release

9   Threshold/gate to endings and completion with potential for new fully informed beginnings

After spending some time looking at the flow of energy as it moves from one number to the next, go back to **Chapter Ten: Kether** and reread the poem of that sphere.

APPENDIX TWO

The 32 Keys of Wisdom

Path	Hebrew Name/Letter	Meaning	The Sphere(s) of Connection

The Paths of Pure Essence 1 - 10

Path	Hebrew Name/Letter	Meaning
1	Kether	Crown
2	Chokmah	Wisdom
3	Binah	Understanding
4	Chesed	Mercy
5	Geburah	Might
6	Tiphareth	Beauty
7	Netzach	Victory
8	Hod	Glory
9	Yesod	Foundation
10	Malkuth	Kingdom

The Paths of Synthesis 11 - 32

Path	Hebrew Name/Letter	Meaning	The Sphere(s) of Connection
11	Aleph	Ox	Kether - Chokmah
12	Beth	House	Kether - Binah
13	Gimel	Camel	Tiphareth - Kether
14	Daleth	Door	Binah - Chokmah
15	Heh	Window	Chokmah - Tiphareth
16	Vau	Nail	Chokmah - Chesed
17	Zayin	Sword	Binah - Tiphareth
18	Cheth	Fence	Binah - Geburah
19	Teth	Serpent	Chesed - Geburah

Path	Hebrew Name/Letter	Meaning	The Sphere(s) of Connection
20	Yod	Hand	Chesed – Tiphareth
21	Kaph	Palm of the Hand	Chesed - Netzach
22	Lamed	Ox-Goad	Tiphareth - Geburah
23	Mem	Water	Geburah - Hod
24	Nun	Fish	Tiphareh - Netzach
25	Samekh	Prop	Tiphareth - Yesod
26	Ayin	Eye	Tiphareth - Hod
27	Peh	Mouth	Hod - Netzach
28	Tzaddi	Fish Hook	Netzach - Yesod
29	Qoph	Back of the Head	Netzach - Malkuth
30	Resh	Head	Yesod - Hod
31	Shin	Tooth	Malkuth - Hod
32	Tau	A Cross	Malkuth - Yesod

The next volume of this series, *Awakening the Paths*, will provide more detail on the Paths of Connection – the 11th – 32nd.

Bibliography

Ashcroft-Nowicki, Dolores. *The Shining Paths*. Leicestershire, England: Toth Publications, 1983.

Butler, W.E. *Apprenticed to Magic and Magic and the Qabalah*. Northhamptonshire, England: The Aquarian Press, 1978.

Denning, Melita and Phillips, Osbourne. *Magical States of Consciousness*. St. Paul, MN: Llewellyn, 1985.

Denning, Melita and Phillips, Osbourne. *The Serpent and the Sword, 2nd Edition*. St. Paul, MN: Llewellyn, 2005

Fortune, Dion. *The Mystical Qabala*, Revised Edition. Boston, MA: Red Wheel/Weiser, 2000.

Goddard, David. *Tree of Sapphires*. York Beach, ME: Weiser Books, 2004.

Gray, William. *Qabalistic Concepts*. York Beach, ME: Weiser Books, 1997.

Gray, William. *The Ladders of Light*. York Beach, ME: Weiser Books, 1981.

Kliegman, Isabel. *Tarot and the Tree*. Wheaton, IL: Quest Books, 1997.

Knight, Gareth. *A Practical Guide to Qabalistic Symbolism*. Boston, MA: Red Wheel.Weiser, 2001.

Parfitt, Will. *The Elements of the Qabalah*. Elements Books Limited, 1991.

Regardie, Israel. *A Garden of Pomegranates*. St. Paul, MN: Llewellyn Publications, 1970.

Regardie, Israel. *The Middle Pillar, 2nd Edition*. St. Paul, MN: Llewellyn Publications, 1985.

Stewart, R.J. *The Miracle Tree*. Franklin Lakes, NJ. Career Press, 2003.

Trobe, Kayla. *Magic of Qabalah*. St. Paul, MN: Llewellyn Publications, 2001.

Wang, Robert. *Qabalistic Tarot*. York Beach, ME: Weiser Books, 1983.

About the Author

Robin Fennelly is a third degree initiate within The Assembly of the Sacred Wheel Tradition and is High Priestess of Oak and Willow Coven within the ASW. Her spiritual journey is strongly rooted in both Eastern philosophy and the Western Magickal systems from which she has formed a core foundation that is diverse in knowledge and rich in spiritual practice.

As a teacher of esoteric studies, she has used Astrology, Hermetic Qabala, Numerology, and Tarot as the foundation of her diverse selection of workshops and writings for more than 20 years. Robin has written articles for The Witches' Voice online community, The Esoteric Tymes E-Newslettter and her blog, The Magickal Pen. She is author of *It's Written in the Stars* (Astrology) the First Volume of **The Inner Chamber** series and *A Weekly Reflection: Musings for the Year*.

Robin is the owner of Holistic Embrace services for mind, body and spirit and provides services such as Tarot readings, Astrology reports, Serenity Nights and other related offerings. She lives in Eastern Pennsylvania and her life is blessed by a 35-year marriage, five children, 2 pets and the opportunity to work in the field of public education.

Contact Information

Website: robinfennelly.com
Email: oawhighpriestess@yahoo.com

Books by Robin Fennelly

The Inner Chamber: Volume One
It's Written in the Stars
A Study of Astrology
First Edition: November 2012

The Inner Chamber: Volume Two
Poetry of the Spheres
A Study of the Qabalah
First Edition: November 2012

A Weekly Reflection
Musings for the Year
First Edition: November 2012

Future Volumes in The Inner Chamber Series

Awakening the Paths
An exploration of the Qabalistic Paths of the Tree of Life

A Walk Through the Major Arcana
A Study of the Major Arcana of the Tarot

The Midnight Flame
Solar and Lunar Mysteries and Magick

The Sacred Vessel Mysteries
Esoteric Studies and Western Hermetics

Awakening the Energetic SELF
Energetic Practice and Protocol

Vessel Of Light

An Exploration of Consciousness and SELF -Awareness